"Rock Gymnastics. The strain on the fingers is extremely severe. In fact the climb, as it is, approaches the limit of strength, and were it two feet longer I question whether it would not be beyond the powers of any man"

Claude E Benson on the difficulties of climbing Matterhorn Arete at Almscliff in 1908.

Yorkshire Gritstone Bouldering
Steven Dunning and Ryan Plews

Written and Designed by
Steven Dunning and Ryan Plews

Published by Total-Climbing Ltd 2008

© Total-Climbing Limited 2008

Cover Photo, Alex Messenger

All rights reserved. No part of this publication may be reproduced, stored in a retrieval system, or transmitted in any form or by any means, electronic, mechanical, photocopying or otherwise without prior written permission of the copyright owner.

ISBN: 0-9557508-0-9

www.total-climbing.com

Dave Sutcliffe at Almscliff: Steve Dunning

Contents

5	Foreword	40	Brimham	226	Slipstones
	Warning		Outlying Areas	238	West Vale
6	About the Guide	94	Caley	244	Whitehouses
			Roadside		
7	Grades		Caley Crag	246	Widdop Area
					Widdop Plantation
8	History Timeline	138	East/West Chevin		Widdop Crag
14	Rules of Engagement	144	Earl Crag		Scout Crag
					Dove Stones
16	Yorkshire Weather	170	Hitching Stone		Clattering Stones
	Conditions	174	Ilkley		Gorple
			Rocky Valley		Scout Hut
17	Best Time to Visit		Swastika Stones		Mytholm Steeps
20	Map of Yorkshire		Pub Quarry	290	Woodhouse Scar
22	Almscliff	204	Shipley Glen	308	Notes

James Ibbertson at Almscliff: Steve Dunning

Foreword

The crags in this guide arguably offer the best bouldering in the UK in settings that are generally beautiful and only very occasionally ugly. Collected here are all of the major grit crags excepting those on Barden Moor and Fell. These crags are included in Yorkshire Gritstone Bouldering (Volume 2).

For generations these small outcrops have been the playground of boulderers and the passing of their hands and feet can be felt when climbing many of the problems recorded here. Almscliff has long been the forcing ground for Yorkshire bouldering and along with Caley and Earl epitomise the very best that this country has to offer. However, this guide has 29 crags in total, from the popular to the obscure such as Almscliff and Scout Hut, thus comradeship and solitude can be sought in equal measure. Despite being close to major conurbations the rocks included rarely see the crowds that the Peak District crags receive and whilst this guide is advertising their merits the sheer number of high quality venues should spread the load.

So here it is, a guide to Britain's finest, enjoy it but cherish it and treat it with respect if the pleasure is to continue.

Warning

Bouldering, spotting and any other form of climbing are dangerous activities that carry a risk of personal injury, paralysis or even death. Participants in these activities need to be aware of, and accept, that these risks are present and they should be responsible for their own actions. This book is a reference tool for experienced climbers and is not intended as an instruction manual. The information in this book is unverified, the authors and publisher can not accept responsibility for its accuracy, nor are they liable for any injuries or damages to participants or third parties that may arise as a result of its use.

About The Guide

Eliminates

This guide would have been roughly the size of a breeze block had we decided to try and describe all the eliminates. We have decided to only include significant eliminates of historical importance. Obviously you may feel that your eliminate has been harshly omitted and it warranted inclusion. Well you can't please everyone.

New problems

Any new problems or even thoughts on grades and descriptions can be recorded at www.Yorkshiregrit.com a superb resource that allows you to upload videos and pictures as well as post comments and grade suggestions. This will allow future publications and updates to remain as accurate as possible.

Approach and access

The inclusion of a climbing area within this guide does not necessarily guarantee that you have a right to climb there or even a right to access the crag. Access to crags constantly changes if in any doubt please refer to the Regional Access Database on the Access and Conservation pages of the British Mountaineering Council (BMC) website as this resource provides up-to-date information of any access issues including seasonal restrictions. www.thebmc.co.uk.

Areas not covered in this guide

Due to the vast number of bouldering areas it was not practical to include every crag in either volume. However, **www.total-climbing.com** has many of the omitted crags available as free pdf downloads. Another excellent resource is **www.yorkshiregrit.com**. Bridestones has suffered more than any other crag in Yorkshire. The amount of erosion and the rate at which the erosion has accelerated in recent years is quite shocking. We decided that it was best to 'rest' Bridestones and include some new venues to help take the strain.

Volume 2

This book contains all the superb crags situated on Barden Fell and Barden Moor with a number of other "high and wild" venues. Indeed crags such as Lord's Seat, Crookrise and Simon's Seat offer some of the finest bouldering in the country. The book is available from February 2008. These crags deserve a separate guide, such is the variety and volume of quality on offer. For those in the know it is clear that the major developments in the future will be on these fine crags. Also, it saves you having to carry a 600 page guide as it's unlikely that you would visit crags in both guides on the same day.

Grades

After much deliberation we decided to go with the font system as it appears to be better understood by the majority of modern boulderers and has fewer limitations when compared to the V grade. The grade table will help those who are unsure and have used different systems.

Traverses are treated no differently to 'up' problems (unlike in fontainebleau) an 8a traverse being just as hard as an 8a up problem. You may discover that you walk up one 7a only to spend ages flailing on another. Remember, bouldering on gritstone is highly specific to the height of the participant. The lack of mega steep problems and the abundance of technical walls and slabs tends to favour the taller climber.

V Grades

Font Grades

V0-	V0	V0+	V1	V2	V3	V4	V5	
3	3+	4	4+	5	5+	6a	6a+ 6b	6b+ 6c 6c+

V6	V7	V8	V9	V10	V11	V12	V13	V14	V15
7a	7a+	7b	7b+ 7c	7c+	8a	8a+	8b	8b+	8c

Colour Symbols have been used to indicate problems in the following grade boundaries

We have also used a star symbol to indicate problems of outstanding quality

*

- 🔵 3 to 5+
- 🟡 6a to 6c+
- 🔴 7a to 7c+
- 🟢 8a to 8b

V0-V10
100+ problems

theLEEDSwall

Funky volume problems
Slabs & vertical walls
Steep boards
& Roofs

Open 7 days a week
Equipment Shop & Cafe
www.theleedswall.co.uk
100a Gelderd Road, Leeds LS12 6BY
0113 2341554

History Timeline

Problem	The Crucifix	Matterhorn Ridge	Angle Allain	Teaspoon Variation	Le Joker
Grade	5	4+	5+	6a+	7a
First Ascent	Unknown	Claude E Benson	Pierre Allain	Arthur Dolphin	Robert Paragot
Area/Place	Almscliff Yorkshire	Almscliff Yorkshire	Fontainebleau	Almscliff Yorkshire	Fontainebleau
Date	1900	1908	1934	1948	1953
Comments	Exact date not known but certainly early in the 20th century.	It is still great now even after 100 years of hands and feet polishing it.		This grade indicates the ability of Dolphin who sadly died aged only 28.	

YORKSHIRE GRITSTONE BOULDERING

Morrell's Wall	Crease Direct	The Villain	The Thimble	Syret's Roof	Horror Arete
5+	6a	6a	6c	6c	6c
Mike Drysdale	Allen Austin	Don Whillans	John Gill	John Syret	Barry Rawlinson
Almscliff Yorkshire	Crookrise Yorkshire	Bridestones Yorkshire	Black Hills South Dakota	Almscliff Yorkshire	Bridestones Yorkshire
1956	**1957**	**1959**	**1961**	**1972**	**1974**
Named after Tom Morrell who had tried but failed to climb it.		Whillans climbed this three times in one evening and offered a pint to anyone who could do the problem, the money stayed in his pocket.	Perhaps this is Gill's most famous problem but not his hardest, he possibly climbed up to 7c+. He was the founding father of modern bouldering, chalk innovator and training guru.	Systematic climbing wall training resulted in many hard problems for Syret. This one is hard, highball and with a last move crux that has smashed the heel of at least one world champion!	

History Timeline

Problem	Ron's Cracks	Red Baron	Desert Island Arete	The Big Three	Vim
Grade	7a/7a+	7a+	7a	8a-8b	6a
First Ascent	Ron Fawcett	Mike Hammill	Jerry Peel	Jim Holloway	Ken Wood
Area/Place	Crookrise Yorkshire	Shipley Glen Yorkshire	Earl Crag Yorkshire	Colorado USA	Shipley Glen Yorkshire
Date	1974	1976	1976	1975/77	1977
Comments	Number 2 is high and hard!	Mike had big arms and a big vision for what gritsone could offer the boulderer.	Named after a game the ascentionist and friends played, "desert island climbs".	The Big Three are Trice, Slapshot and Meathook. Myth and legend surround these problems but whilst the grades are debated the obvious talent of "ahead of his time" Holloway is not.	"This was really the route that started the ball rolling at the Glen and could even be regarded as the start of the bouldering revolution on grit. It showed the way and provoked Al Manson and I to try to climb all the walls and all the aretes at the Glen". Mike Hammill.

Midnight Lightning	The Thatcher Years	Bald Pate Super Direct	Blockbuster	Lay-By Arete	C'etait Demain
7b+	Ungradeable	7b	7b-7c	7b+	8a
Ron Kauk	Maggy Thatcher	Andy Brown	Ron Fawcett	Paul Ingham	Jacky Godoffe
Camp 4 Yosemite	Uk	Ilkley Yorkshire	Caley Yorkshire	Slipstones Yorkshire	Fontainebeau
1978	1979	1980	1982	1983	1984
	The Thatcher years had a great impact on UK climbing standards with many leading activists climbing full-time whilst "signing on the dole".		Just how Ron managed to squash his oversized fingers into such a small hold is a mystery!	This original version climbed the arete on the right before swinging onto its left side.	Fotainebleau's first 8a

YORKSHIRE GRITSTONE BOULDERING

History Timeline

Problem	Walk On By	Fight On The Black	Rock Atrocity	Edge Of Darkness	Careless Torque
Grade	7c+	7b	7c	7c	8a
First Ascent	Rob Gowthorpe	Joe Healey/Jerry Peel	Jerry Moffat	Jerry Peel	Ron Fawcett
Area/Place	Curbar Peak District	Widdop Yorkshire	Parisella's Cave Wales	Earl Crag Yorkshire	Stanage Peak District
Date	1984	1985	1986	1986	1987
Comments		Named after the nail biting finish to the world snooker final between Dennis Taylor and Steve Davis and watched by the first ascentionists the previous night.	Starting in the middle of no where and finishing much the same, this testpiece was ahead of its time in terms of style. Another masterpiece from the master.	Considered by Jerry to be his hardest first ascent.	Only a handful of ascents in twenty years has added to its reputation.

YORKSHIRE GRITSTONE BOULDERING

The Fin/Keel	Superman	Terry	Jason's Roof	Cypher	High Fidelity
7b+/c	8a+	7c	8a	8b	8b
Andy Swan/Dunne	Jerry Moffat	Andy Swan	Jason Myers	Ben Moon	Steve Dunning
Almscliff	Crag X	Caley	Crookrise	Slipstones	Caley
Yorkshire	Peak District	Yorkshire	Yorkshire	Yorkshire	Yorkshire
1988	**1989**	**1990**	**1996**	**2002**	**2003**
Still one of the most sought after ticks in Yorkshire.		One of many contributions by one of the county's finest boulderers.	This audacious line climbs perhaps the best boulder roof on grit!	Another great line stolen by a damned Peakie!!	One of Yorkshire's finest lines succumbed to a prolonged and bold approach.

Rules of Engagement

Crash Pads

Crash pads have revolutionised our approach to bouldering. Pads are allowing us to boulder higher than before, micro-routes are fast becoming modern highballs. The bouldering guide will become thicker and the route guide will become thinner as more and more micro-routes are approached as boulder problems. However, pads can only remove a fraction of the risk and its worth considering that a poorly positioned pad can be more of a hazard than no pad at all. Crash pads also serve to preserve the ground around the base of problems helping to reduce the amount of ground erosion.

Behaving badly

The vast majority of folks who buy this guide will automatically do the right thing when it comes to looking after the bouldering environment which gives us so much pleasure. However, judging by the state that some crags and boulders are left in it would appear that a few people need a gentle reminder.

Chalk and tick marks

Throwing chalk all over a hold ain't going to make it feel any bigger and drawing a three foot long tick mark won't make getting hold of it any easier either. Try and use a limited amount of chalk and get rid of any excess with a rag or brush. Tick marks should be removed in a similar way.

Brushing

Without exception wire brushes should not be used on any boulder. Most boulderers tend to use nylon brushes to remove chalk and moisture from holds. However, many of these brushes (even some of the ones supplied by climbing companies) are very stiff and have a small surface area, as a result of this they create a great deal of pressure on the surface of the rock, eventually resulting in the nature of the hold changing. Unfortunately once the first layer of grit is broken down the rock soon erodes at an alarming rate. The best method is to get into the habit of using a rag to give the hold a gentle wallop, removing excess chalk and moisture.

"Every precaution will, of course, be taken by the punctilious scrambler to avoid making use, as finger-holds, of the initials, names, and flourishes that have been incised on the rock by that part of mankind which never climbs without leaving its mark. Should you inadvertently lay hands on one of these or use it as a toe-scrapper, it is incumbent on you to descend and make a fresh start."

Baker (1903) speaks of climbing a rock with carvings on it

Yorkshire Weather

Visitors to the UK often believe that it does nothing but rain for much of the year, but the statistics tell a different story with much of the UK experiencing similar rainfall to mainland Europe. However, Yorkshire does experience rather unpredictable weather even though rainfall is fairly evenly distributed throughout the year, it is impossible to predict a season that would guarantee everyday climbing. The summer months can bring extended periods of sunshine with gradual increase in humidity which are quickly followed by heavy rainfall. From late autumn through to early spring rainfall is generally lighter, but usually more sustained.

The prevailing winds are from the west and with them they bring much moisture from the Atlantic Ocean. Once this moist air hits the high fells and moors around our crags it cools down and falls as rain. Luckily for us the high Pennine region to the west catches much of the bad weather first and as a result much of the Yorkshire region enjoys low annual rainfall. Of course all of this will mean nothing if you're now sat looking at a soaked crag.

Luckily for us we are blessed with a rock type which is super quick to dry and can allow climbing within an hour of rainfall, providing the crag receives plenty of sun, wind or hopefully both. Clean, lichen free crags with a good degree of exposure such as Almscliff dry very quickly.

Conditions

The best conditions for climbing gritstone are experienced on cold, dry days. This doesn't restrict hard climbing to the winter months it just requires the boulderer to be that bit more 'canny' with crag selection. North facing crags such as Ilkley and Earl can be unbelievably cold on a winters day but from late spring to early autumn they can provide excellent conditions.

Best Time To Visit

January to March: These are the coldest months with a strong possibility of heavy overnight frost and snow fall especially on the Dales themselves. Crags such as Almscliff remain clean and lichen free throughout the winter and catch any available winter sun.

April and May: Starting to get warmer with very pleasant sunny periods, but always the possibility of showers. Crags such as Caley are usually a good bet.

June, July and August: This is the driest period of the year but not the best for experiencing good friction. However, the higher crags can offer good conditions in a spectacular setting. Ilkley and Earl are probably the most exposed north facing crags, offering good summer friction.

September and October: The weather is generally pleasant at this time of year with temperate autumnal days. Conditions can vary a great deal at this time of the year with prime conditions usually arriving sometime during October. Earl crag is superb at this time of the year along with the Widdop area which offers good options if you choose to chase or avoid the sun/wind.

November and December: The nights are now drawing in with the chill of winter starting to show, and the possibility of snow fall. Usually the wetter of the winter months, the fast drying crags such as Brimham and Shipley Glen become very popular.

Daylight Hours

Sunrise in Winter is typically after 8am and sunset is before 4pm, making approximately 8 hours of daylight. In the summer months sunrise is generally around 4:30am and sunset is around 9:30pm, making approximately 17 hours daylight.

At the end of March the UK switches to British Summertime (GMT+1) and clocks are put forward by 1 hour. Be alert to the change to avoid missing flights etc. At the end of October clocks are put back by 1 hour as the UK reverts to Greenwich Mean Time (GMT).

Average Monthly Rainfall (mm)

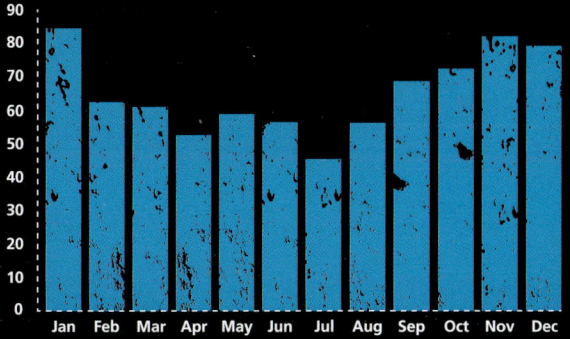

Average Daily Temperatures (°C)

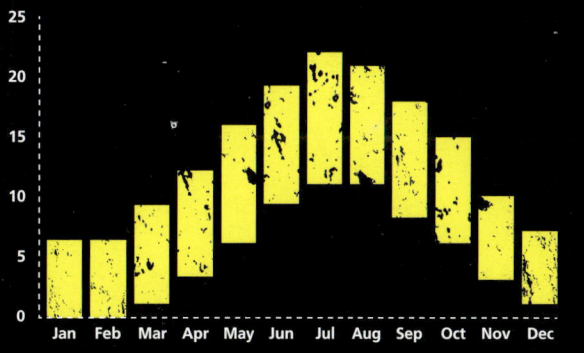

Acknowledgements

Big thanks to the following for their invaluable contributions.

Kevin Avery, Dalvinder Sodhi, Pete Chadwick, Ewan McCallum, Mark Katz, James Ibbertson, Tim Stubley, Nigel Poustie, Tom Peckitt, Dave Cowl, Jon Pearson, Ben Meeks, Dave Buchanan, David Mason, Neil Sugden, Francis Holland, Mark Radtke, Paul Clough, Mike Hammill, Mick Ryan, Alan James, Greg Chapman, Jerry Peel, Dave Sutcliffe and Simon Panton.

A special thanks to John Wainwright for his excellent graded list which served as a solid foundation for the guide. Also Jon Pearson from Yorkshiregrit.com for all his support and assistance.

Photography

A big thanks for the excellent work from the following photographers. Pete Chadwick, James Ibbertson, Alex Messenger, Simon Richardson, Adam Long, Dave Parry, John Coefield, Jon Pearson and Dave Simmonite.

Apologies to anyone we have missed.

Ryan and Steve.

TOTAL-CLIMBING

YORKSHIRE GRITSTONE BOULDERING

Volume 2, February 2008

Photo: Alex Messenger

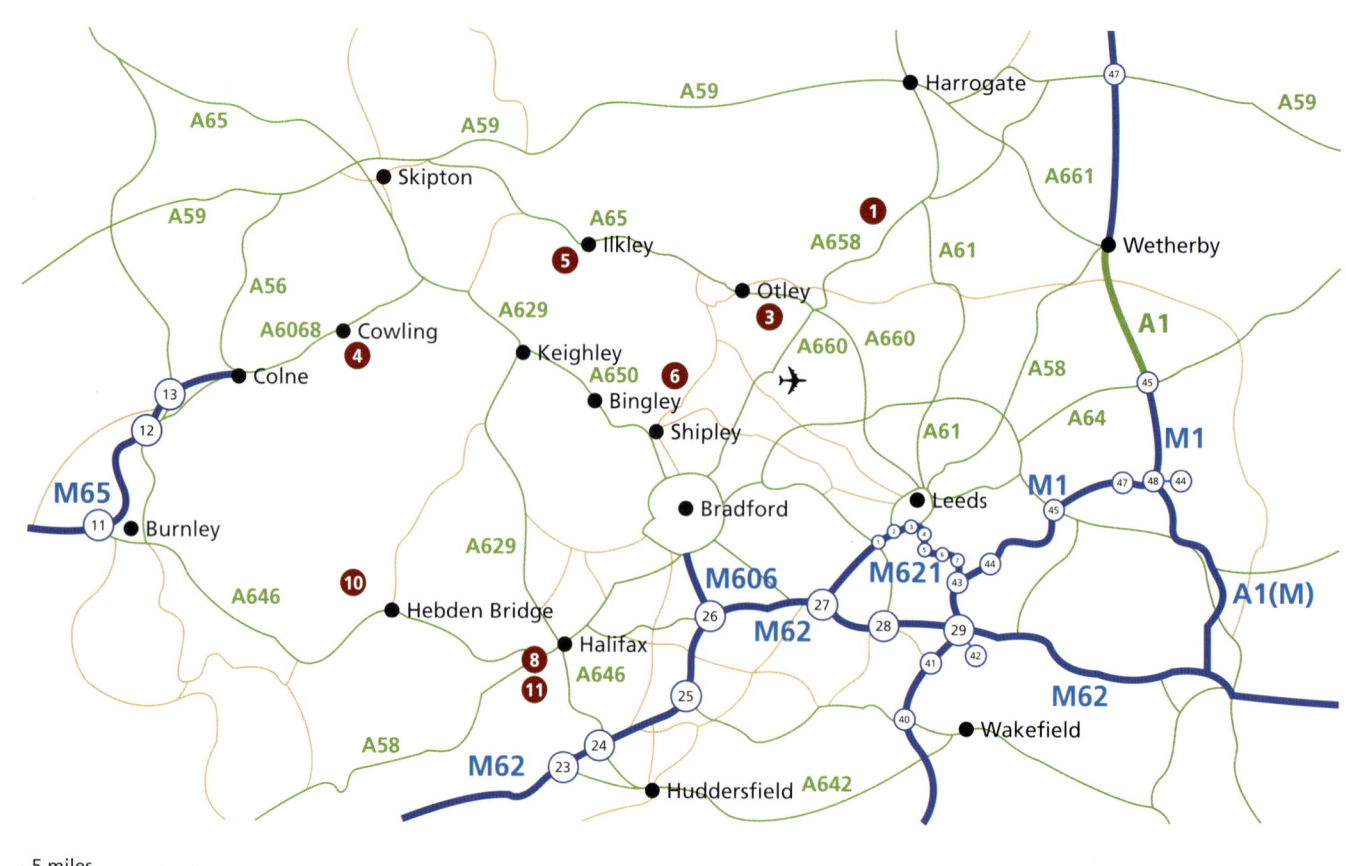

1	Almscliff	7	Slipstones
2	Brimham Outlying Areas	8	West Vale
		9	Whitehouses
3	Caley Roadside Caley Crag East/West Chevin	10	Widdop Area Widdop Plantation Widdop Crag Clattering Stones Scout Crag Dove Stones Gorple Scout Hut Mytholm Steeps
4	Earl Crag Hitching Stone		
5	Ilkley Rocky Valley Swastika Stones Pub Quarry		
6	Shipley Glen	11	Woodhouse Scar

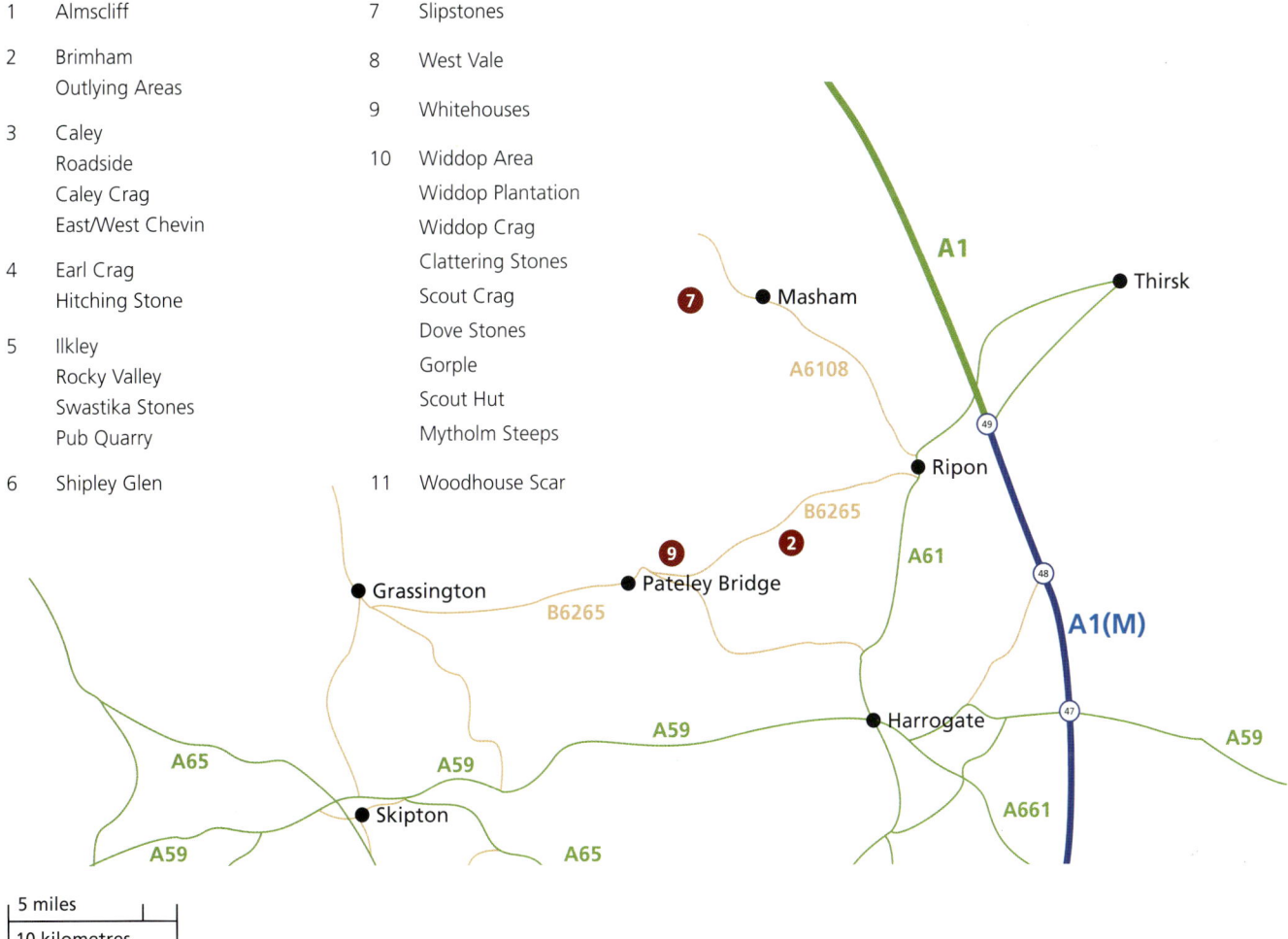

YORKSHIRE GRITSTONE BOULDERING

Almscliff

Almscliff is without doubt the most popular of all of the crags in this guide; it stands high on the northern ridge above Upper Wharfedale and dominates the valley. The crag is split neatly into two, upper and lower tiers of rock, High Man and Low Man. High Man is divided by a large rift in its centre whilst the lower tier is made up of a number of large boulders and the impressive buttress of Low Man. The rock is wonderful compact grit that often supplies positive holds in usually steep settings. Due to its exposed position Almscliff is very quick to dry after rain, however this means there is often a bitter wind to contend with, equally it is not uncommon on a sunny and still winters day to complain of high temperatures causing failure on sought after projects.

The crag has a deserved reputation for working the arms with many of the problems being exceptionally steep however, on close inspection it becomes apparent that Almscliff has it all, monster link-ups, highballs, bald slabs and endless eliminates all of the highest quality. In short, Almscliff is a world-class bouldering venue.

Approach & Access

Approaching from Harrogate on the A659 (Otley-Harrogate Road) take the North Rigton turn-off, drive through the village turning right onto Crag Lane, eventually joining Merrybank Lane, park at the corner lay-by below the western end of the crag. From Pool/ Otley direction turn off the A659 at the Stainburn turn-off. After about a mile Merrybank Lane is reached, turn left and follow this to the corner lay-by described above.

The farmer has asked that climbers avoid the boulders in the field below the main areas. Also, the start of path next to the stile can get extremely muddy, don't under any circumstances climb over the wall to avoid the mud.

N.G.R. SE 268490

ALMSCLIFF

1. Morrell's Wall Group
2. The Virgin Group
3. The Matterhorn
4. The South Cave
5. Black Wall
6. Demon Wall
7. Syrett's Roof
8. Wall of Horrors
9. Heart Shaped
10. Teaspoon Variation

Area 1: Morrell's Wall Group

1. ● (7a+)
From the short arete traverse rightwards on pockets and finish up Morrell's Wall.

2. ● (6a) **Morrell's Wall**
An excellent fingery problem up the crimps on the highest part of the face.

3. ● (7b+) **Slopey Traverse** ✱
Finish up Morrell's Wall. Avoid using heel hooks and the chipped edge for the 7c tick. Link into a reverse of problem 1 (avoiding breaks) to push the grade up to 7c+.

1. ● (7b+) **Fieldside Traverse**

2. ● (5+)
From a sloping hold on the lip, take the easiest line to the top.

3. ● (6c)
A good eliminate, climbing the wall starting on the lay-away and gaston to reach a slopey hold on the slab.

4. ● (5+)
Climb the centre of the face using the obvious big flake on the slab.

1. ● (6c+) **Below the decks**
SDS. Without the block for feet.

2. ● (7b+) **Grape Strain**
From the block at the front of the boulder, traverse left along the lip, around the nose to finish above the overhanging face.

3. ● (5)
SDS. The overhanging face using everything.

4. ● (7c+) **Lasting Satisfaction**
SDS. From the flake move right to the arete and finish over the bulge. Avoid pockets.

"Bouldering is the pleasantest of off-day distractions; but too many men allow themselves to spend the time on the merely difficult. Its use should be for safe exercises on rules of style... To wrestle up pure difficulty, such as you would not attempt in exposed higher climbing, by dint of muscle and strenuosity, proves nothing and does no good; it only reduces the restful value of the off-day."

Geoffrey Winthrop Young (Mountain Craft, 1949)

Area 1: Morrell's Wall Group

1. ● (6c)
   The blunt nose on the large boulder left of Flying Arete requires a confident approach. SDS. 7b+.

2. ● (6a+) **Flying Arete** ★
   Classic arete from Mike Hammill. The right arete is 6a.

Opposite Flying Arete is a superb wall with a number of nice warm-up problems and eliminate traverses.

1. ● (5+)
   The right edge of the central wall.

2. ● (7a) **Barley Mow**
   The highball hanging crack.

3. ● (6a)
   SDS. Juggy moves to a good break, use pocket for left and tiny crimp on arete for right to gain the ledge.

4. ● (6a)
   SDS. From good jug gain the break and use a pocket and small break to slap for a good edge and the top.

5. ● (5) **Pork Chop Slab**
   Technical wall on positive but spaced edges.

Dalvinder Sodhi on Jess' Roof: Steve Dunning

Area 2: The Virgin Group

1. 🔴 **(7c) Stretch Armstrong**
   The left side of the Sewer Rat roof, with a huge reach from the back of the roof to the lip. Finish direct.

2. 🟢 **(8a) Canine**
   SDS. From the flake at the back, into the crimp with your right and undercut with left, slap into slopey pocket with right and go again to good pocket. Finish up the arete.

3. 🔴 **(7b+) Sewer Rat Connection**
   Start on jug under roof climb around lip to pocket and jug.

4. 🔴 **(7b+) Top Cat Traverse**
   Traverse R-L the line of pockets above the lip, around arete, then keep low on slopers smd swing into the crack.

1. 🟡 **(6a)**
   The overhanging wall passing good holds via stiff pulls.

2. 🟡 **(6c+)**
   Traverse the break rightwards to finish up the nose.

3. 🟡 **(6b+)**
   From the boulder climb the lip of the roof.

4. 🔴 **(7b+) Underhand**
   The left edge of the roof, climbed from a sit-start at the back. 7c if you traverse left from the jug on the lip and pull over the roof.

5. 🟡 **(6a)**
   The hanging arete from standing.

Area 2: The Virgin Group

The Virgin

This enormous boulder has plenty of hard, highball problems on the two overhanging walls, and a few easier problems on the slabby back wall.

1. ● (6b+) **Virgin Traverse**
   Starting with hands and feet on the block. Finish in the corner.

2. ● (8a) **Gaskins Problem**
   Step off the block and use the vertical crack and a poor scoop/pocket to gain the break.

3. ● (8a+) **Cherry Falls**
   From the break gain the edge with your right and use the pocket out left to jump for the break.

4. ● (7b)
   From the break, reach a small crimp in the wall with the left hand, then use the slanting crack to reach the break. Jump off.

5. ● (7b) **Crusis** ✱
   SDS. Up to break and reach the slopey side of the slanting crack. Slap up this to break. Originally finishing up the wall above. 7a+ if you jump off at the break.

6. ● (8a) **The Full Virgin Traverse**
   Start on the east (slabby) face. Traverse L-R down the hill onto The Virgin face and traverse the top break to the arete. Reverse The Gypsy to join the Virgin Traverse. Finish back on the east (slabby) face.

7. ● (6b) **The Gypsy** ✱
   The right arete starting on the good break with a committing finish up and right. Finishing leftwards up the face is The Fox 7b.

8. ● (7b+) **Virgin Extension Traverse**
   Technical traverse from groove round the arete to easier ground. Linking from the Virgin Traverse is 7c.

9. ● (7c+) **Magnum Opus Super direct**
   From small pocket on lip of roof, into press and stand up. Either jump off or finish up Magnum Opus. Using the big pocket is 7c.

10. ● (7c+) **Dick Hymen**
    Start in the groove, traverse up and right, finishing with jump for big pocket on Magnum Opus.

Area 2: The Virgin Group

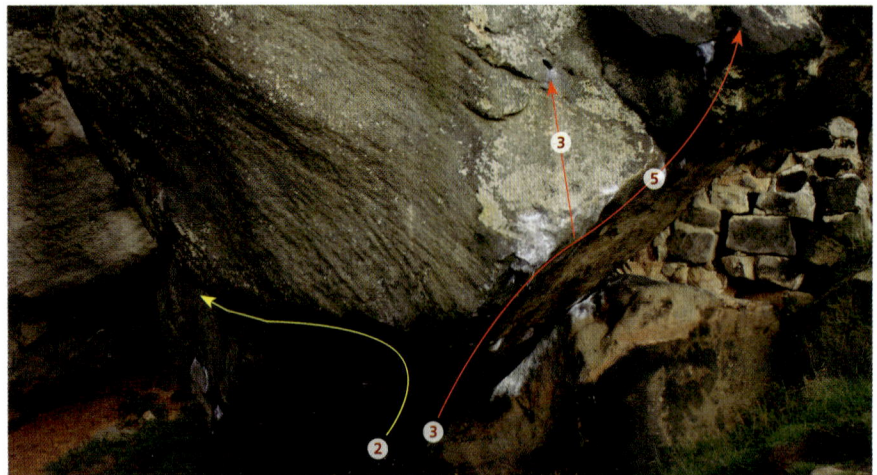

1. ● (6a)
   The undercut arete on the left side of the roof.

2. ● (6c) **In Limbo**
   From the back of the roof reach around the lip to finish up the pockets. The crack is out. The crack from SDS. is **6b+**.

3. ● (7c) **The Keel/Fin** *
   A classic problem climbing out from the back of the roof via a chipped hold on the lip.

4. ● (7c+) **The Real Keel**
   The Keel without the chipped hold.

5. ● (7c+) **The Bulb**
   Start at the back of the roof as for The Keel. Reach the lip then use a bulbous hold to reach good holds and the top. Also 7c+ if you avoid the chip.

6. ● (8a) **Keelhaul**
   Reverse C&A Traverse into The Keel without the block at the back of the roof.

7. ● (8b) **Real Keelhaul**
   As the name suggests. Link keelhaul into the Real Keel.

8. ● (7b+) **Natural Traverse**
   From the nose, traverse the sloping lip rightwards into the gully, finishing along Sloper Patrol.

9. ● (6b+) **Burnell's Traverse**
   Left to right traverse to join the end of the C&A Traverse. Often dirty.

10. ● (6b+) **C&A**
    From the back of the roof, climb out via the break into the crack. Traverse left to finish up the left arete via a good jug.

10. ● (7c)
    Reverse C&A into the Keel.

11. ● (8a+) **Lip Service**
    Link problem 10 into The Bulb. Finish by reversing Sloper Patrol.

12. ● (8a) **All Natural**
    C&A traverse into Natural Traverse keeping low under The Keel/Fin.

Area 2: The Virgin Group

Area 3: The Matterhorn

1. ● (6c+) **Sloper Patrol**
   The slopey lip traverse is a classic. Climbed going downhill but much better in the other direction.

Unnamed Boulder
A small boulder opposite Sloper Patrol has a few good lower grade problems.

2. ● (5+)
   The left side of the arete.

3. ● (5)
   The right side of the arete passing some nice moves.

Ed's Dyno
A small block opposite The Keel boulder with a few problems on the vertical front face.

1. ● (6c+)
   Traverses the lower break of the boulder from right to left. Finish slapping for the top.

2. ● (7a) **Ed's Dyno**
   Dyno off two small crimps.

3. ● (5+)
   Thuggy moves from the good ledge passing breaks to the top.

The Matterhorn
A big pinnacle at the foot of Low Man.

1. ● (5)
   A crimpy (and reachy) little problem up the left side of the smooth wall left of Matterhorn Ridge.

2. ● (7a+) **Fractal**
   The smooth wall, starting at an undercut.

3. ● (4+) **Matterhorn Ridge** *
   Highball classic. The SDS makes a hard move to the slopey break. Finish up Matterhorn Ridge 7b+.

4. ● (8a) **Chaismata**
   Highball clamping with a poor landing.

Area 3: The Egg

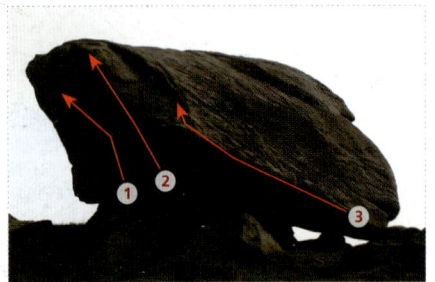

The Egg
Lots of eliminates and link-ups exist here. The classics are described.

1. ● **(7b+) Matt's roof**
   Big slap to a good crimp on the left side of the severely overhanging face.
2. ● **(7b+) Buffy wants daddy**
   Right of Matt's Roof, slap directly for a dish at the top. Right arete is out for hands.
3. ● **(7b+) Streaky's Traverse**
   Desroy's classic bum-scraping traverse.
4. ● **(8a) Zen**
   Links Streaky's Traverse into Matt's Roof.

1. ● **(6c+)**
   The left arete of the pocketed side of the egg, from a sit-start.
2. ● **(7b+) Pistol Whip**
   The shallow groove in the wall. Highball.

Many variations exist on the Egg Boulder see www.Total-climbing.com for more information.

Between the Egg and South Cave is a small block with a couple of problems. **Steve's Wall** is the short wall climbed from a sitter at 7a+. Also, below the Egg boulder is a small pinnacle **Three Way Boulder** with a good problem passing a flake up the long slab, around 6a from standing and 6C from a SDS. The steep side has a nice juggy 5.

Area 4: South Cave

1. ● **(7a) Patta's Arete**
   The excellent blunt arete. Start from crimps on the lip, or (better), from the slab down on the right.
2. ● **(6a+)**
   The arete is good, with a long reach for the break.

1. ● **(6b)**
   A one move wonder.

Photo: Alex Messenger

Area 5: Black Wall

Area 6: Demon Wall

Black Wall

The impressive wall at the right end of the upper tier over the dry stone wall.

1. ● **(6b+)**
   From the wall, traverse rightwards across the break to the arete.

2. ● **(7a) Dreamland**
   The centre of the smooth steep slab next to the wall. The SDS. is **7b+**.

3. ● **(6a)**
   The arete next to the corner. Avoiding the pocket is **6c**.

1. ● **(5) The Crucifix** ✱
   The obvious hanging crack. SDS. Avoiding the break is a **6b** tick.

2. ● **(6a) Crucifix Arete**
   The obvious arete is excellent.

3. ● **(6c) Pebble Wall** ✱
   The classic pebble pulling wall.

4. ● **(7b) Pebble Wall Variation**
   The right side of Pebble Wall, reachy.

5. ● **(7a) Crucifix Traverse**
   Eliminate. Traverse the lip of the roof below the big break from left to right.

Area 6: Demon Wall

Demon Wall Roof

The horizontal roof left of The Crucifix has some classic problems and numerous eliminates.

1. ● (7b+) **Stu's Roof Left-Hand**
   Starting just left of Stu's roof. Use big undercut to walk feet around wall to the left. Finish up Stu's Roof.

2. ● (7c+) **Stu's Roof**
   The roof just left of Demon Wall Roof on small crimps. Starting at a small flake climb into undercuts and slap around on small crimps.

3. ● (7c) **Demon Wall Roof Left-Hand**
   Avoid the break and finish up left using a painful ear and sloper.

4. ● (7a+) **Demon Wall Roof** ✱
   Climb the middle of the roof using the obvious flake to reach the big horizontal break. The best finish is straight up the centre of the wall above. Avoid the break for a 7b+ tick.

5. ● (7c+) **Hot Dog Fromage**
   The roof between Demon Wall Roof and Dolpin Belly Slap. Stretch from undercuts at the back of the roof to the good hold on the lip and jump for the break.

6. ● (7a) **Dolphin Belly Slap**
   The edge of the roof left of the corner crack. Another classic involving crafty technique.

8. ● (8a) **Dialectics**
   Start with both hands on the arete of Dolphin Belly slap, cross the roof longways without using the back wall or the lip of the roof and finish as for Stu's Roof.

9. ● (8a) **The Exorcist**
   Start as for Dolphin Belly Slap, traverse left on lip and finish up Demon Wall Roof Left-Hand. Continuing traversing and finishing up Stu's roof is harder but still 8a.

Ted Kingsworth on Dolphin Belly Slap: Alex Messenger

Area 6: Demon Wall

1. 🟡 (6b)
Sit-start over the bulge.

2. 🟡 (6b)
Climb the roof via the jugs.

Area 7: Syrett's Roof

Area 8: Wall of Horrors

1. ● **(7a) Brown's Roof**
   The extremely highball roof left of Syrett's Roof and right of the gulley.

2. ● **(6c) Syrett's Roof** *
   The central line through the roof. Excellent climbing, with a high and scary crux.

3. ● **(7a+) Si's Arete**
   A tricky little problem up the rounded arete from a sit-start.

Jess' Roof
Above the Syrett's Roof area is a large cave half-way up the crag. Access the problem by scrambling up the gulley left of Brown's Roof.

4. ● **(7c) Jess' Roof** *
   Climb the roof from the back to a hard move at the lip. Escape at the break.

1. ● **(6a)**
   The right side of the arete. Just using holds on the left side of the arete pushes it up to 7a.

2. ● **(7a)**
   The wall right of the arete via two poor holds.

3. ● **(7a+)**
   The bulge immediately left of Wall of Horrors, finishing at the big jug.

4. ● **(6c) Wall of Horrors traverse**
   L-R. From the chimney, traverse right under Wall of Horrors and the niche, finish on the ledge.

5. ● **(6a+) Wall of Horrors**
   The right side of the arete to the jug. Jump off!

1. ● **(7b) The Dark Side Of Chi**
   The prow left of the Parson's Chimney with a less than ideal landing. The crack is avoided.

2. ● **(6c)**
   The middle of the often green wall right of Parson's Chimney.

Area 9: Heart Shaped

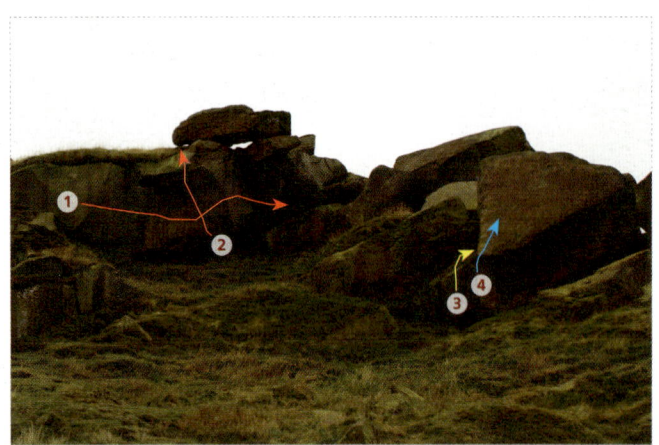

1. ● (7b)
   L-R traverse starting on the slab and finishing under the small roof right of the crack.

2. ● (7b)
   SDS. From the pocket under the roof climb the wall via the lay-aways.

3. ● (6a+)
   Traverse the shelf and pull out onto the slab.

4. ● (5+) **Heart Slab Arete**
   Tricky mantle onto the slab.

1. ● (5)
   The shallow groove passing pockets on the slab.

2. ● (4)
   The slabby arete.

3. ● (7a)
   Low level traverse avoiding the lip and finishing up problem 6.

4. ● (6a)
   SDS. Tricky pull into the groove.

5. ● (4+)
   Rock onto the slab using the pocket.

6. ● (6a+)
   The short but technical arete.

Area 10: Teaspoon Variation

Left of the main crag and next to the stone wall is a small cave with lots of eliminates and the Classic Teaspoon Variation at 6a+.

Naomi Buys on Demon Wall Roof: Alex Messenger

BRIMHAM ROCKS

Toby on Fantasy League: Simon Richardson

Brimham

Situated between Pateley Bridge and Ripon, Brimham Rocks is one of the most popular bouldering venues in Yorkshire. Without a doubt more boulders exist here than at any other venue with the strange and amazing rock formations covering more than 50 acres of Brimham Moor. Set at an altitude of 300m the crag has fantastic views across Nidderdale and offers a wonderful family day out with good grassy areas making the crag child friendly. Not all of the rock lends itself to climbing with the rock quality ranging from excellent to very soft so expect to do a bit of stomping around. The problems tend to be as varied as the rock formations with lots of long traverses, technical walls as well as rounded powerful challenges. The main area of Brimham can be come overrun during the weekends and the summer holidays with hoards of tourists, giving a good opportunity to venture away from the main crag and explore some of the outlying areas where solitude is guaranteed.

Approach and Access

Brimham is without doubt the most complex area within this guide. With many years experience of navigating around the scattered boulders it can still be extremely frustrating finding specific areas. In order to make navigation easier we have split Brimham into a number of areas and provided maps and more detailed descriptions where necessary.

Note

The rock at Brimham is very soft and prone to rapid erosion. Don't climb on damp rock and under no circumstances attempt to wire brush and/or excessively clean the rock.

N.G.R. SE 209637

BRIMHAM ROCKS

1. Pommel Area
   Cubic Block

2. Woodland Area
   The Edge

3. Black Chipper
   Duggies Dilemma

4. Druids Idol

5. The Niche
   The Blacksmith
   Flower Pot Rock
   Dogs Head

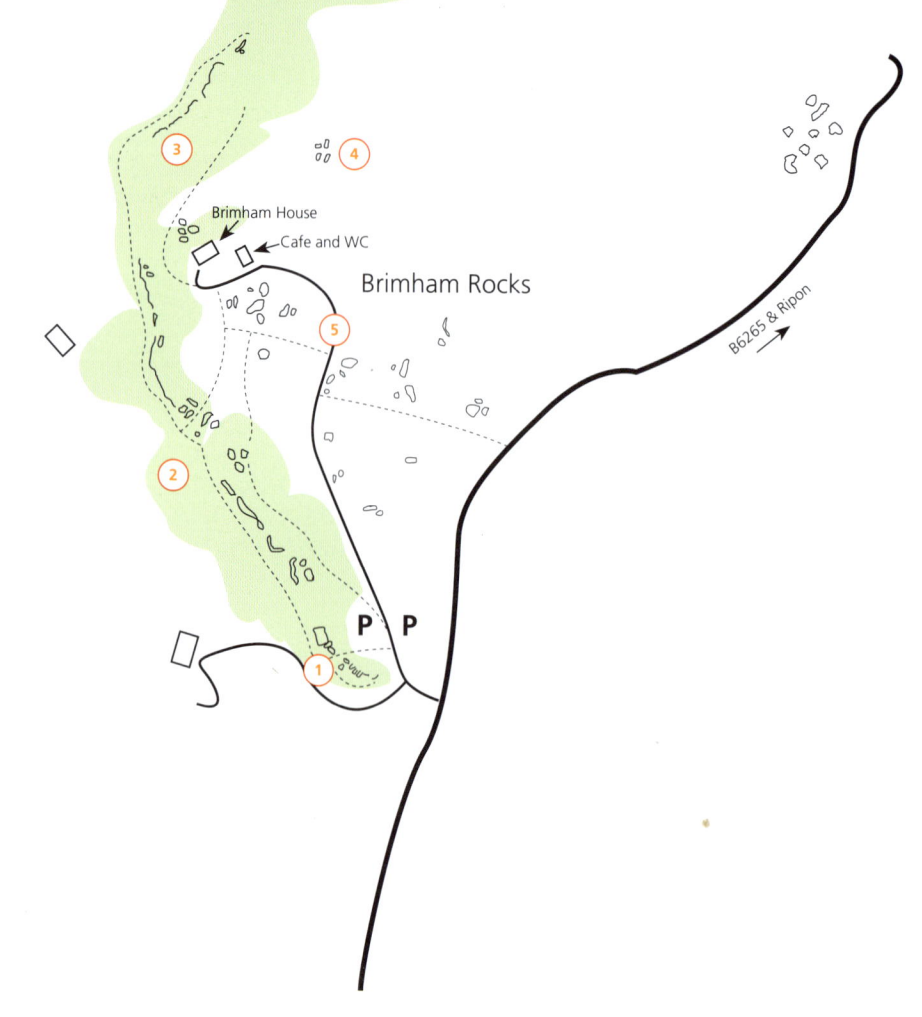

Pommel Area

Less than a minutes walk from the car park the Pommel Area is easily the most accessible area at Brimham. The problems are some of the best in the area with lots of quality rock and in most cases good landings. The climbing is varied with roof problems sitting next to technical walls and aretes.

Cubic Block

Cubic Block is another area close to the car park that offers excellent bouldering. The huge block has problems on two sides the severely overhanging Joker's Wall offers weatherproof bouldering with lots of biceps busting power problems alongside some mega traverses. The front side is less steep and has some excellent technical challenges.

1.1 Pommel Roof
1.2 The Pommel
1.3 The Anchor
1.4 Joker's Wall
1.5 Cubic Block

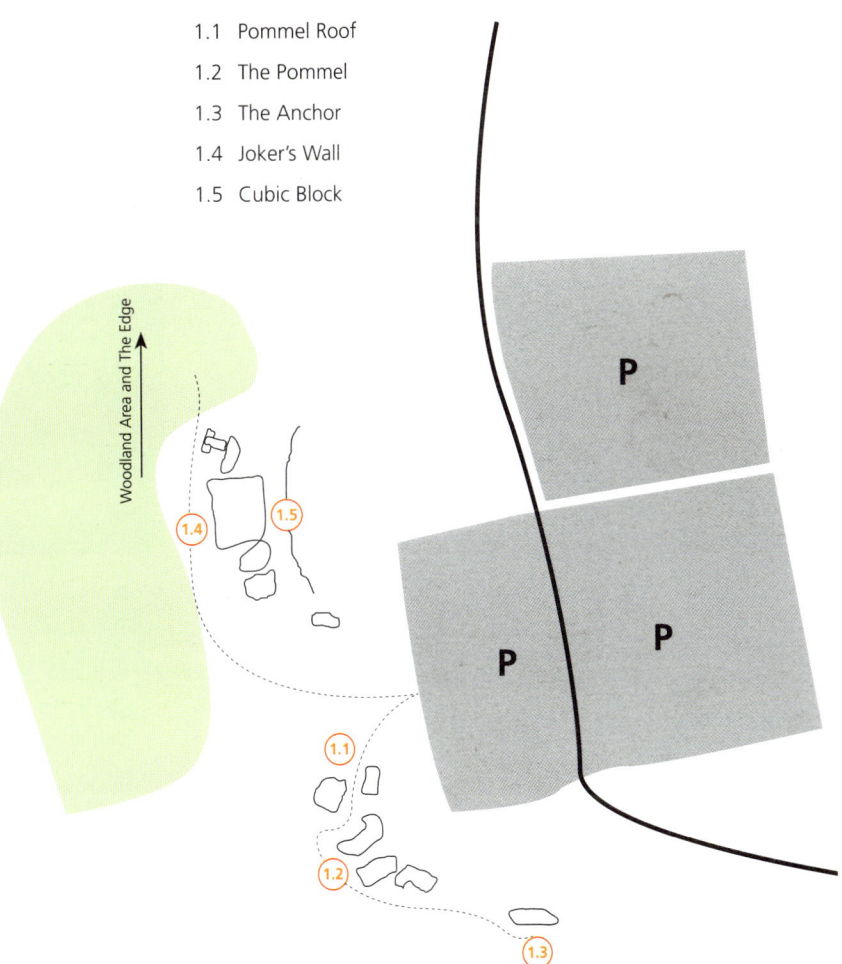

Area 1.1: Pommel Roof

1. ● (6c)
   Traverse the wall L-R under the roof. Finish up problem 6.

2. ● (6b)
   Traverse L-R using holds in the roof. Finish up problem 6.

3. ● (6b+)
   Low start on the break. Climb the roof passing the hole.

4. ● (7a+)
   Traverse L-R across the break, out over the roof, passing slopers on the lip.

5. ● (6c)
   Start on good hold. Climb the right side of the roof and finish passing the flake.

6. ● (5+)
   The wall on the edge of the roof.

7. ● (6c)
   The wall right of the roof.

The wall opposite is home to a classic eliminate 6a+ the break is out.

1. ● (4+)
   The left arete.

2. ● (4+)
   The wall passing the small overlap.

3. ● (4)
   The wall between the overlap and blunt arete.

4. ● (4+)
   The blunt arete.

5. ● (4)
   The wall between the two arete problems.

6. ● (3+)
   The small arete.

The prow opposite is home to a nice problem up a obvious groove passing some slopey breaks.

Area 1.2: **The Pommel**

1. ● (4+) **Gully Arete**
The arete in the back of the gully.

2. ● (6c) **Black Dog Arete**
The butch arete with a slopey top-out.

3. ● (7b+)
The centre of the wall very dynamic.

4. ● (7a+)
SDS. The hanging flake. Much harder than it looks.

5. ● (7a)
SDS. The wall from a sitter using the pocket and eliminating the break.

6. (Pumpy)
Any number of traverses of the bottom break exist finishing up various problems.

1. ● (6b) **The Pommel**
The superb arete is a classic.

2. ● (7b) **Serpico**
From the sloper on the right move up and left to finish up The Pommel.

3. ● (7b) **Benchmark**
From the break use the sloper to gain the slopey top-out.

4. ● (6c+)
The right arete with a desperate mantle.

5. ● (7a+)
Start low on crimps and climb the wall past slopey edges left of the breaks. Super low start off bad edges is 7b+.

6. ● (5+)
SDS. Excellent problem passing the good breaks.

Louise warming up at the Pommel area: Steve Dunning

Area 1.3: The Anchor

1. ● (7a+) **The Anchor**
   From a ledge at the back of the roof move out via pockets to a hard reach for the top. Hard mantle finish.

2. ● (7b+) **Pieces Of Eight**
   The central line avoiding the pockets out right. Much easier for the tall.

3. ● (7b)
   SDS. Gain the left arete, traverse right to join problem 1.

Area 1.4: Joker's Wall

1. ● (6c) **Joker's Wall Arete**
   The steep arete. Escape at the second break.

2. ● (6c+) **Joker's Wall Traverse**
   Traverse the wall from L-R. Either finish up the crack or problem 6 at 7a. Another variation follows the lower line of pockets and finishes up problem 6. 7c+/8a.

3. ● (8a+) **Ironside**
   Follow problem 2 passed the crack, dropping low on pockets before moving around the corner and into the far niche.

4. ● (8a) **Slapstick**
   SDS. Desperate wall passsing the crimp and sloper to the ledge.

5. ● (6a+) **Joker's Wall Left**
   The steep wall just right of the arete. Escape at the second break.

6. ● (6a) **Joker's Wall Start**
   Thuggy moves to the hole and the break. Escape.

7. ● (6b)
   SDS. From the flake climb the wall left of the crack.

www.sypeland.com

Sypeland Outdoors • 23a High St • Pateley Bridge
North Yorkshire • HG3 5AP • Tel: 01423 712922

Area 1.4: Joker's Wall

8. ● (7c+) **Fred Under Ten's**
The wall left of the flake passing the broken edge. Unrepeated since the demise of a hold.

9. ● (6c+)
Powerful climbing up the obvious flake the SDS. is 7a+.

10. ● (8a) **Upside Your Head**
Just right of the blunt arete climb the wall passing a poor side-pull. Unrepeated since hold broke.

11. ● (6c)
SDS. The crimpy wall left of the roof.

12. ● (6b+)
SDS. The wall under the roof passing a layaway.

13. ● (6c+)
SDS. Undercut arete without the good hold or break.

Area 1.5: Cubic Block

1. ● (6a)
   SDS. Feet on plinth move out to arete and a big lock for the break. **The Fridge** avoids the break at 7c+.

2. ● (7b)
   SDS. L-R traverse passing pinch on arete along lip to right arete.

3. ● (6b)
   SDS. Left-hand crack.

4. ● (7b+)
   SDS. The slopey crack finishing up the arete.

5. ● (6c)
   SDS. The arete via the pocket.

6. ● (6a) ✱
   From the flake attack the bulging wall passing slopers. SDS. 6b+.

7. ● (7c) **Snapdragon**
   SDS. Up to sloper on the lip, traverse right to finish up arete.

8. ● (7b+)
   The overlap via some serious locks. Committing.

9. ● (7a)
   The hanging right arete. Nasty landing.

Opposite Cubic Block is a problem that appears to exist half way up a route.

1. ● (7c) **The U Tube**
   Start undercutting the back of the block. Climb out avoiding the side wall.

The undercut arete (6a) below and opposite this problem is well worth a look. Follows the diagonal break to the arete.

Woodland Area

The next area is contained in the wooded area next to Cubic Block that eventually opens out into a clearing. Not the easiest area to navigate but problems such as Happy Days/ Acme Wall and the Rack are classics and well-worth seeking out.

The Edge

The dense woodland area begins to peter out, a clearing opens up revealing the prominent Cleft Buttress. This buttress is home to a number of excellent problems, especially noteworthy is the classic tussle of Pair In A Cubicle and the delicate Murky Rib. Further on the buttresses grow significantly containing much worthwhile bouldering below the Lovers Leap area.

2.1 Hole In The World
2.2 Acme Right
2.3 Acme Wall
2.4 The Green Nose
2.5 Happy Days
2.6 No Red Tape
2.7 Cleft Buttress
2.8 Rachel's Box
2.9 Lovers Leap

Area 2.1: Hole In The World

Area 2.2: Acme Right

1. ● (7a)
From thin holds at the back throw for the lip and into the hole. Either sit in the hole or top-out.

2. ● (6a)
The wall right of the arete passing a pocket.

3. ● (6c)
Thin R-L traverse under roof finishing on break above groove.

4. ● (7a+)
Reverse problem 3 into problem 1.

1. ● (6a+)
The hanging buttress is home to a superb problem on excellent rock. Starting on the juggy ledge move left to a good pocket, make a big lock to an edge and match. Escape at the break.

Photo: Simon Richardson

Area 2.3: **Acme Wall**

1. ● (6b+)
   The thin wall just right of the corner.

2. ● (6c)
   Highball wall with less than ideal landing.

3. ● (6a) **Acme Wall** ✸
   Excellent wall requiring good technique and a committed approach.

4. ● (6c)
   R-L traverse along the break and finish up problem 1.

5. ● (6c)
   SDS. From under the roof climb passing the nose.

6. ● (7a) **The Rack**
   Massive move from break to break.

1. ● (6b+)
   SDS. The quality arete is harder than it looks.

2. ● (5+)
   Delicate slab just right of the arete.

3. ● (3+)
   The centre of the slab.

Area 2.4: The Green Nose

Area 2.5: Happy Days

1. ● (7b)
   SDS. Start with feet jammed in the back break.

1. ● (7b) **Happy Days** ✳
   L-R traverse under the roof pulling round the roof to finish up the groove. Escape left at the break.

2. ● (7c) **Ian's Traverse**
   L-R traverse across the lip of the roof to the jug. Finish up problem 1.

3. ● (8a) **The Fonze**
   Link Happy Days into the right arete by traversing right across the poor pockets. Finish up problem 5.

4. ● (8a+) **Mr C**
   Link Ian's Traverse into the Fonze.

5. ● (6c) **Bilge Pump**
   The right arete requires nifty footwork.

6. ● (6c)
   The roof left of the niche from the break at the back of the roof.

Area 2.6: No Red Tape

1. ● (7b+) **Red Tape Traverse**
   L-R traverse along the break passing the prow to a tricky rock-over around the corner.

2. ● (5+)
   Clean wall on good edges.

3. ● (5+)
   Centre of the wall.

4. ● (7a+)
   SDS. From under the roof gain the good edge on the lip and make a hard rock-over (via a pebble) leftwards.

5. ● (7a+)
   SDS. From under the roof move up and right to finish right of the prow.

Photo: Simon Richardson

Area 2.7: Cleft Buttress (Left)

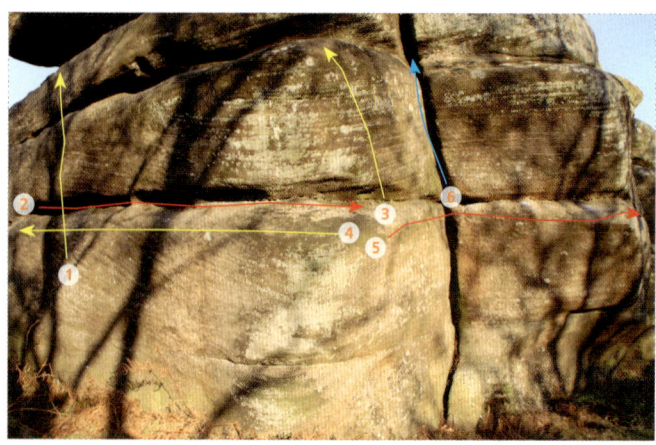

1. 🟡 **(6c)**
   The rounded break leads to a committing move on nasty slopers above.

2. 🔴 **(7a)**
   Pumpy L-R traverse following the slopey break. Finish up the rounded arete of Clingon.

3. 🟡 **(6c) Clingon**
   The rounded arete left of crack. Escape from the ledge.

4. 🟡 **(6b+) Murky Way Kid**
   From the arete traverse the break leftwards and finish up the far arete.

5. 🔴 **(7a) Jumper's Traverse**
   L-R traverse of the break all the way around the arete to finish along problem 8. For an even more pumpy challenge link problem 2 into the start at 7b.

6. 🔵 **(5+) Mirky Way**
   The nasty crack.

John Coefield on The Titfield Thunderbolt: Dave Parry

Area 2.7: Cleft Buttress (Right)

7. ● (7a)
Big dyno from sloper to break.

8. ● (6b) **Murky Rib**
The classy arete climbed on the left side. SDS. 7a.

9. ● (6a)
Traverse the rising break between both aretes.

10. ● (7a) **Cleft Arete**
SDS. The arete climbed on the right side. 5+ from standing.

11. ● (6b) **High Steppa**
The wall passing the pockets.

12. ● (5+) **Green Arete**
Technical and awkward arete.

13. ● (5) **Perverts Crack**
The nice curving crack.

14. ● (7a) **Pair In A Cubicle** ✱
From the undercut make use of some nasty slopers to a beastly top-out.

15. ● (7a+) **Governor**
The wall just right is even harder.

16. ● (7c+) **Jim's Problem**
SDS. The seldom repeated roof passing the open undercut pocket to a desperate mantle.

17. ● (7b+) **Thelma**
The rounded bulge just right of Jim's Problem.

18. ● (7a+) **Pablo**
From low holds use a crimpy sidepull to throw for the slopey break and finish direct.

19. ● (7b)
R-L traverse along the slopey break. Finish up problem 14.

Chris Kay on Black Chipper Arete: Steve Dunning

Area 2.8: Rachel's Box

1. ● **(7a+) Rachel's Box**
   SDS. From the undercut use a flake to climb rightwards. Finish up the nose.

2. ● **(6c+) Triangular Roof**
   SDS. From the undercuts move out leftwards passing the pocket.

3. ● **(7c) The Archer**
   SDS. Starting super low climb the lip to finish up problem 2.

Area 2.9: Lovers Leap

1. ● (5+)
   The left arete is often grotty.

2. ● (5)
   From the ledge move left to the top. Nice.

3. ● (5+)
   From the jug move right and finish up the arete. Excellent.

4. ● (6a) **Trackside arete**
   The arete direct from standing. Climbed on the right side is worth 6b.

5. ● (4+) **Trackside Left**
   The left side of the lovely slab.

6. ● (5) **Trackside Right**
   Technical problem taking the rightward line on the slab.

7. ● (4) **Heart Arete**
   The right arete.

1. ● (6a) **Tight Fit**
   SDS. Starting on the right climb the excellent arete.

2. ● (5) **Orange Crush**
   The hanging crack.

3. ● (6b+) **Anniversary Arete**
   The excellent right arete of the crack.

4. ● (5+)
   The clean slab passing the pockets to the break.

5. ● (6a)
   The rounded arete climbed on the left side.

6. ● (6b) **Mono state**
   The right side of the arete.

Above and right is a crack in the roof (half-way up the crag).

7. ● (7c)
   SDS. The crack in the roof is super thuggy.

Black Chipper

Beyond the Lovers Leap area just passing the prominent pinnacle it is possible to drop down to the Black Chipper area. Such classics as Whisky Galore 7a and The Titfield Thuderbolt 7b sit next to the excellent arete of Ritornal 6a+.

Duggies Dilemma

This area is home to a small selection of problems most of which are highball with the exception of a couple of nice traverses. Mustard 7a+ is an awesome problem with a high crux passing a mono.

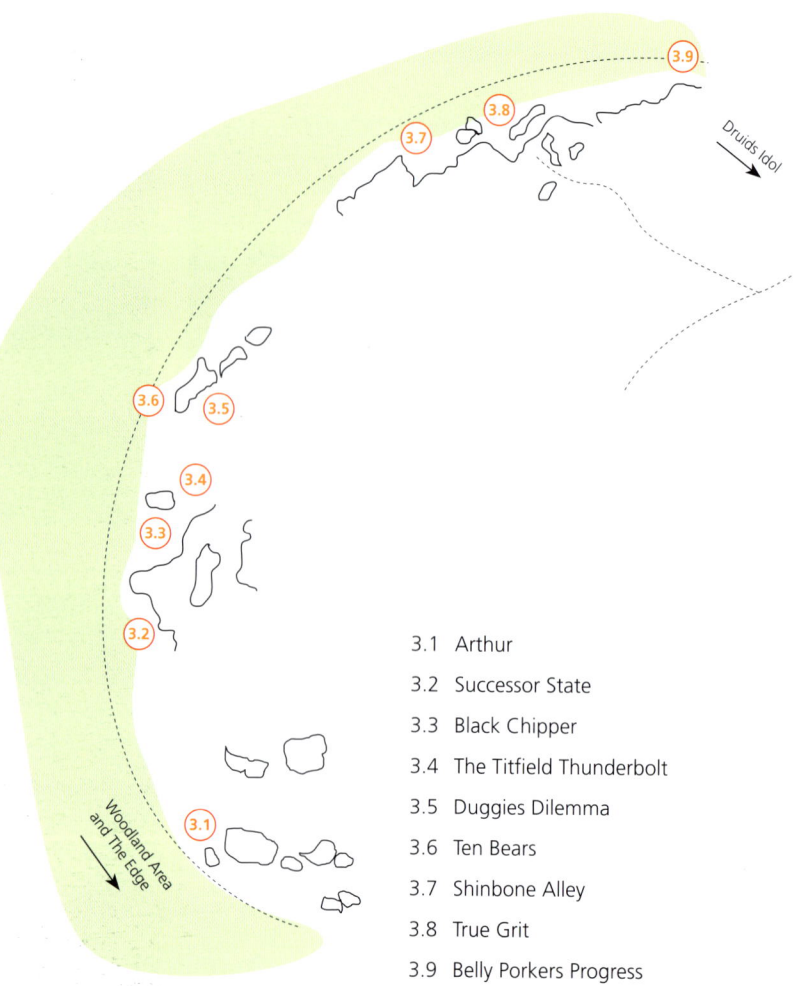

3.1 Arthur
3.2 Successor State
3.3 Black Chipper
3.4 The Titfield Thunderbolt
3.5 Duggies Dilemma
3.6 Ten Bears
3.7 Shinbone Alley
3.8 True Grit
3.9 Belly Porkers Progress

Area 3.1: Arthur

1. 🟡 (6c+) **Arthur** ⭐
   Excellent highball wall. Follow the slopers direct into the large hanging undercut. Finish rightwards.

2. 🔵 (4+) **George II**
   The right-hand side of the wall passing some good flakes.

John Coefield on Bilge Pump: Dave Parry

Area 3.2: Successor State

Area 3.3: Black Chipper

1. ● (5+)
   The hanging arete.

2. ● (4+)
   The centre of the wall on good holds.

3. ● (7a) **Successor State**
   The excellent highball arete. Dodgy landing.

4. ● (7b+)
   The centre of the wall avoiding both aretes. Bold.

5. ● (6a+) **Ritornal**
   Another quality highball arete. The crux is near the top.

1. ● (4+) **Black Chipper**
   The rib left of the arete.

2. ● (7a+)
   L-R traverse around the arete, across the wall, onto the slab and around the far arete.

3. ● (6b)
   The left side of the arete.

4. ● (4+)
   The awkward crack.

5. ● (6a)
   Thin wall just right of the crack.

6. ● (5+) **The Arch**
   The wall climbed direct to the arch. Escape left.

7. ● (6a)
   The rounded arete is high but quality.

Area 3.3: Black Chipper

Area 3.4: The Titfield Thuderbolt

1. ● (7b) **Black Chipper Arete**
Start one hand on the sloper and the other on the low undercut.

2. ● (7c) **Black Chipper Low**
Low start to problem 1 starting on the right at a good flake.

3. ● (7b) **Parrapper The Rapper**
The SDS. to the arete just passing the leaning boulder is a quality problem.

1. ● (7c) **Chicken**
From the edges gain a poor sloper and throw for the top.

2. ● (7b+) **The Titfield Thuderbolt** ✱
Awesome wall with a dynamic finish. SDS. 7C.

3. ● (7a+) **Pussy Galore**
The vague arete requires clean footwork.

4. ● (7a) **Whisky Galore** ✱
The groove is a fine problem one of the best in the area.

Area 3.5: Duggie's Dilemma

Area 3.6: Ten Bears

1. 🟡 **(6a) Spare Rib**
The left arete is a superb highball challenge.

2. 🔴 **(7b) Mustard**
The right arete above the crack. The left arete is avoided.

3. 🟡 **(6b+) Spring Roll**
The centre of the wall starting up the crack.

1. 🟡 **(6a)**
SDS. The left arete has some thuggy moves on nice holds.

2. 🟡 **(6c+) Ten Bears**
SDS. From the right arete (hand on flake) traverse leftwards to finish up problem 1. Keeping super low on poor pockets is 7b.

Area 3.7: Shinbone Alley

Area 3.8: True Grit

Area 3.9: Belly Porkers Progress

Below Dougies Dilemma is a superb slopey traverse.

1. ● (7a+) **Shinbone Alley**
   SDS. L-R traverse on slopey holds and finish with a tricky mantle.

1. ● (6b) **True Grit**
   The superb steep crack is a classic struggle. Escape from the ledge.

2. ● (7b+) **True Romance**
   The centre of the steep wall inside the chimney. Starts low on edges with a big slap to a good edge. Mind your head on the block behind.

1. ● (7c)
   Start up the steep prow before swinging around leftwards from the pinch. Finish up the steep wall and escape leftwards.

2. ● (7b) **Belly Porkers Progress** *
   The steep prow with a committing rock-over onto the thin slab. Either escape or solo the rest of an E6.

Druids Idol

This area offers a mixed bag to the boulderer. Much of the rock has an overly sandy nature and considering the number of blocks much of it offers little in the way of quality problems. However, there are a number of exceptions and for those willing to quest around, a few classics are hiding amongst the greenness.

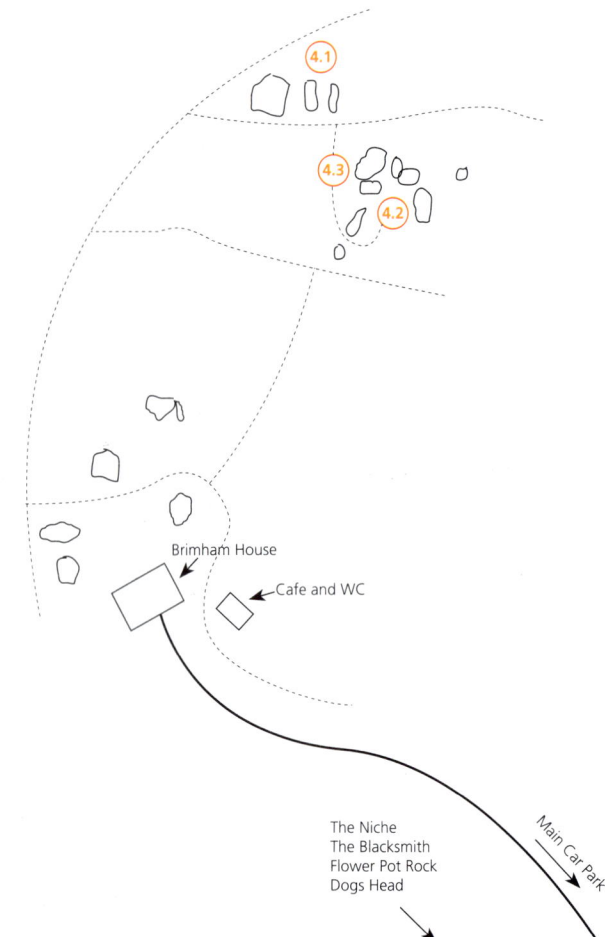

4.1 The Yoke Of Oxen
4.2 Pinky Boulder
4.3 The Bay

Area 4.1: The Yoke Of Oxen

1. ● (7c) **The Grouch**
   SDS. From the block attack the prow via some serious compression moves.

2. ● (7b) **Borne Again**
   SDS. From the block climb the off-width crack.

3. ● (7c) **Pounce**
   SDS. From ledge on the right climb the bulging prow with a desperate finale.

4. ● (7c+) **Ponce**
   SDS. From the ledge climb the faint line of slopers right of the prow. Another desperate top-out.

Dave Cowl on Pounce: Steve Dunning

Ceri Lewis climbing in The Blacksmith area: Kevin Avery

Area 4.2: Pinky Boulder

Area 4.3: The Bay

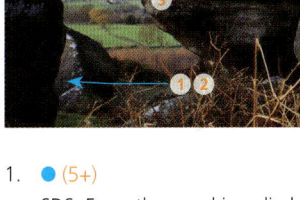

1. ● (8a) **Pinky** ✱
SDS. Desperate start to get established on slopers. Finish direct. The standing start is 7a+.

2. ● (7c+) **Pinky Traverse**
Traverse L-R starting on the slopers at the left-hand end of the break and finishing using the good flake before the arete. Extending this to finish around the arete is 7c.

3. ● (8a)
SDS. Start as for problem 1 and traverse the slopers rightwards passing a flake to finish around the right arete. Finishing via the large flake is 7c+.

4. ● (7c)
SDS. Hard moves up to the slopers before finishing up the arete direct.

1. ● (5+)
SDS. From the good jug climb the hanging prow passing slopers on the wall.

2. ● (5)
The pocketed slab right of the rippled wall.

3. ● (7c+) **Mike's Problem**
The spectacular hanging arete starting on the break.

4. ● (5+)
Take a direct line up the wall without using the arete.

5. ● (5)
The clean-cut arete. SDS. 5+.

The Niche

Finally an area that is easy to find due to its proximity to the main path. The Niche has a variety of problems from thin and desperate leaning walls to rounded aretes and a monster traverse. Some problems stay dry during light rain, however, after heavy rain a small lake tends to form at the base of the traverse line.

The Blacksmith/
Flower Pot Rock/Dogs Head

This jumble of boulders straddles either side of the main track a couple of minutes from the main car park. The Blacksmith has the best selection of problems, although some of the rock is starting to deteriorate. Fantasy League is a superb 7a+. Flower Pot Rock is on the same side of the track to The Blacksmith yet the rock tends to be a lot greener. Opposite these areas is Dogs Head home to a couple of good problems but not very extensive.

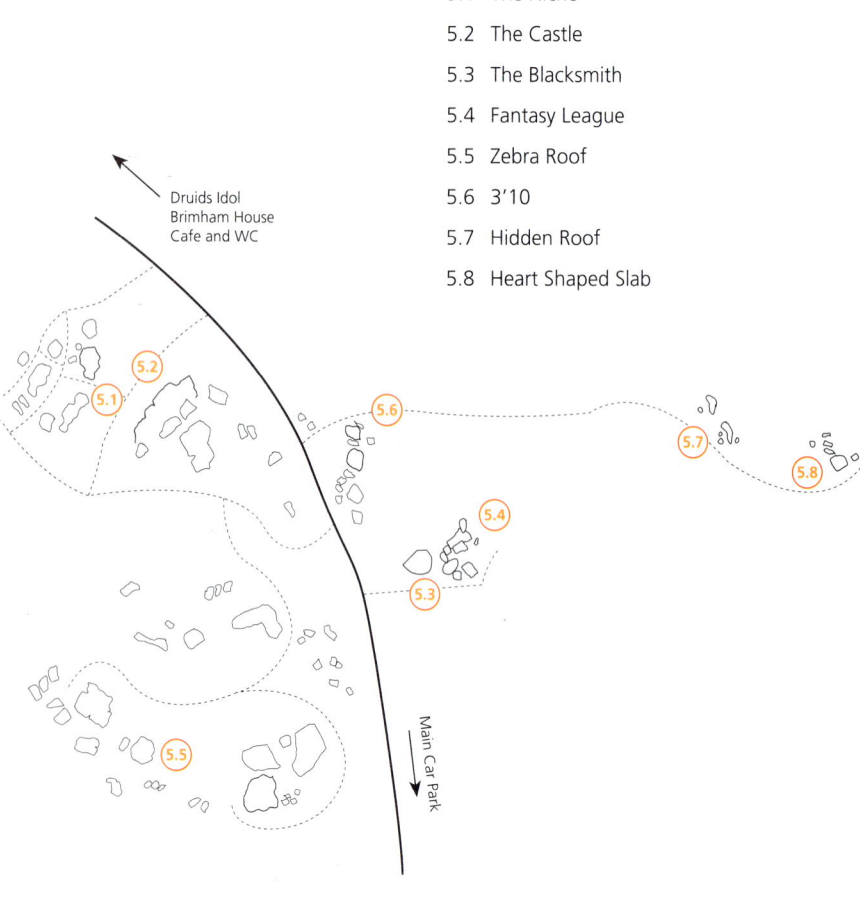

5.1 The Niche
5.2 The Castle
5.3 The Blacksmith
5.4 Fantasy League
5.5 Zebra Roof
5.6 3'10
5.7 Hidden Roof
5.8 Heart Shaped Slab

Area 5.1: The Niche

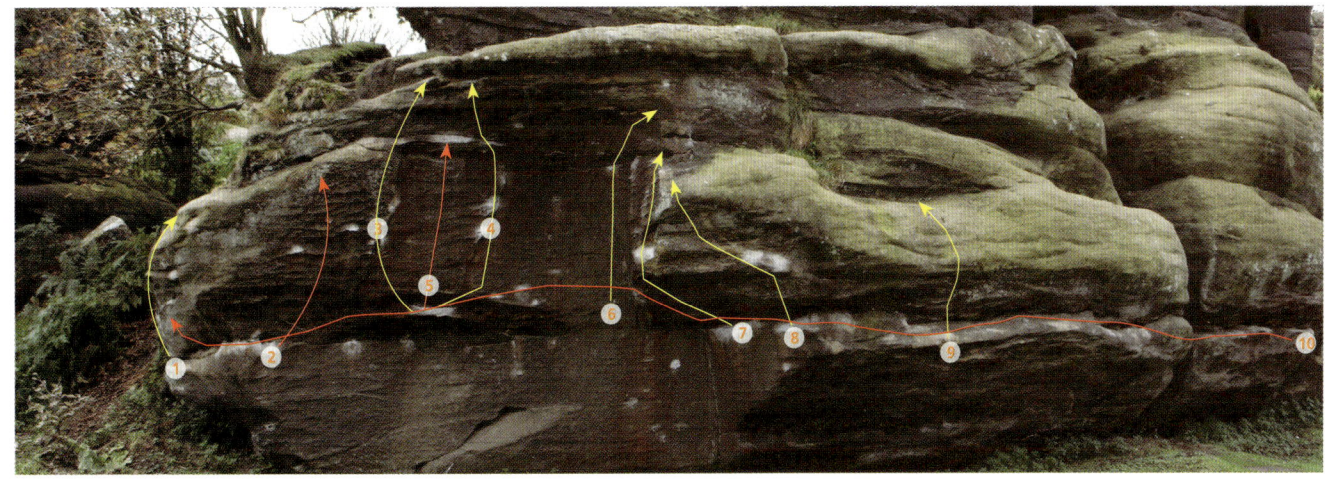

1. 🟡 **(6c) Niche Arete**
   SDS. The blunt arete passing slopers from the break. Double dyno from the break to the top 7a.

2. 🔴 **(7a+)**
   The wall between the arete and the flake, starting from the low break.

3. 🟡 **(6a)**
   The left-hand crumbly flake. Eliminate the starting jug for a 7a tick.

4. 🟡 **(6a)**
   The right-hand flake.

5. 🔴 **(7c) Jumper's Dyno**
   The huge dyno from the low jug to the break. Allegedly this has been done to the top (up and right?).

6. 🟡 **(6b+) Niche Corner**
   The left wall of the corner passing a small pocket, moving right at the roof.

7. 🟡 **(6b) Niche roof**
   Start at a big hold under the roof, slap up left to crimps on the lip, then right to a large pocket.

8. 🟡 **(6b)**
   Gain the finish of the previous problem via slopey holds on the vague arete.

9. **(?) Niche Mantle**
   Desperate mantle problem.

10. 🔴 **(7b) Long Haul** ✶
    The R-L traverse. Start on the juggy break right of the crack. Traverse left crossing the niche under the roof to finish up problem 1.

Area 5.6: 3'10

1. ● (7c+) **3'10**
   The short powerful bulge. Requires lots of compression strength.

1. ● (7b) **Andy's Traverse**
   Very condition dependant traverse. Starting on the left of the boulder, traverse rightwards to the right arete. Rock-over leftwards to finish.

Area 5.7: Hidden Roof

Area 5.8: Heart Shaped Slab

1. ● (7a+) **Hidden Roof Traverse**
Cool traverse under the roof from L-R.

2. ● (5)
The bulging left arete of the crack.

3. ● (4)
The right side of the crack finishing up and right.

4. ● (6a+) **Hidden Wall**
Nice wall problem starting at a good lay-away and utilising a long reach.

1. ● (5) **Just Jump**
The wall left of the slab.

2. ● (6b+) **Just Do It**
Start at a layback hold and climb the left edge of the slab.

3. ● (5) **Heart Mantle**
Tricky mantle onto the slab.

4. ● (6c+) **Heart-Shaped Slab**
From the undercuts on the wall right of the slab, slap up the arete and onto the slab.

BRIMHAM OUTLYING

Dave Cowl climbing at Crimpy Roof: Steve Dunning

Brimham Outlying

Many of the finest problems in the Brimham area can be found on the superb boulders and edges situated on the periphery of the main crag. The rock here tends to differ in character at each venue and ranges from bullet hard grit offering crimpy lines to softer, more heavily featured rock that requires a subtle, technical approach.

Hare Head

Crimpy Roof

Crimpy roof has some excellent problems on good quality rock. You need to be climbing at least 7b to get any joy here but those operating at this level and above will find plenty to keep them occupied. Much of the climbing may appear a little eliminate on first acquaintance but don't let this fool you, problems such as To Me To You 7c+ and To You Too 8a are superb.

Harvey

The low roof of Harvey is the closest boulder to the road although it's not easily visible. The problems tend to be predominantly on slopers and rounded edges. Unfortunately some of the rock is a bit soft but overall the climbing is good, especially Harvey 7a+ which is a classic.

Dolphin Nose

The north side of the large tower has some excellent challenges on good quality rock. The problems tend to be very crimpy which is unusual for Brimham. Problems such as The Big Green 7a and Dolphin Nose 6c+ are of great quality.

Approach and Access

The best approach is to follow the track which runs parallel to the road from the main car park. Don't park on the verge.

1. Crimpy Roof
2. Dolphin Nose
3. Harvey

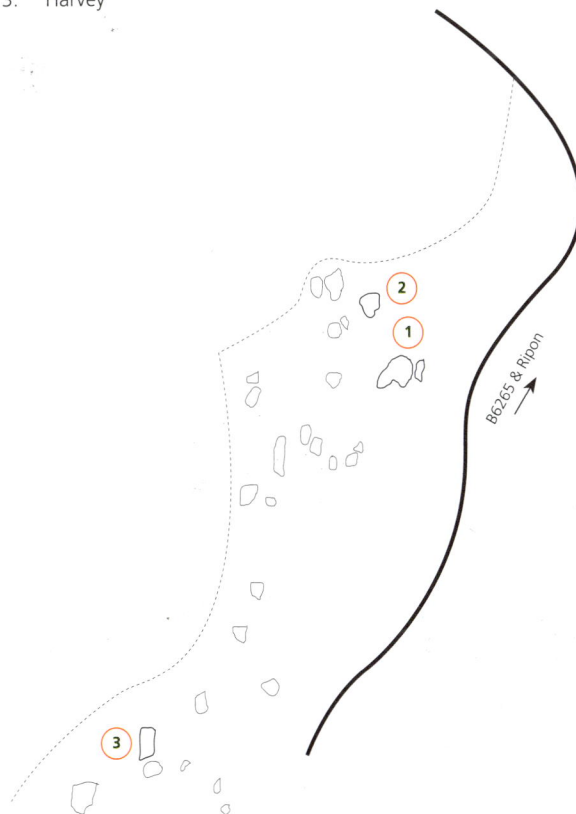

Area 1: Crimpy Roof

Crimpy roof offers some of the best hard climbing at Brimham on arguably the best rock. All problems described start very low at the back of the roof.

1. ● (7c+) **To Me To You**
   From the back of the roof climb out passing crimps to finish up the rounded arete.

2. ● (8a) **To You Too**
   Extend problem 1 finishing up slopers right of arete.

3. ● (7b+) **Crimpy Wall**
   Climb out of the roof to the crimps and slap for the break.

4. ● (7c) **Claret**
   Start hanging the poor holds right of the arete, traverse left to finish up problem 3.

Dave Cowl on Crmpy wall: Steve Dunning

Area 2: Dolphin Nose

Area 3: Harvey

1. ● (6a+)
   SDS. The left arete trending left on slopers.

2. ● (7c)
   L-R traverse along the middle break on poor edges.

3. ● (6c)
   The low L-R traverse from the arete to finish on the good holds on the right arete.

4. ● (6c+) **Dolphin Nose**
   Sit start at the hole, go straight up on small crimps and finish up the flake on the arete to the right.

5. ● (7a) **The Big Green**
   From the low shelf link into problem 4.

6. ● (6a) **Dolphin Arete**
   The arete passing the dodgy flake.

This next buttress is a short walk over the brow of the moor. Follow the path until a broken buttress becomes clear down to the left.

1. ● (6c)
   Start low on broken crimp and edge under roof, move up and right.

2. ● (7b) **Harvey**
   SDS. The wall past the slopey blobs. Excellent.

3. ● (7a+) **Elwood P Dowd**
   SDS. Slightly easier wall just to the right.

4. ● (7c)
   From the start of problem 4 move left and finish up problem 2.

5. ● (7c)
   Desperate L-R traverse of the slopey break.

Bat Buttress

Bat Buttress is the collection of boulders next to a farm just beyond the main Brimham car park when travelling towards Summerbridge. The crag consists of a clean, large buttress and a long, low roof. The climbing here has a sunny aspect and as a consequence the rock dries quickly. Stand out problems such as The Riddler 6b+ and All Guns Blazing 5+ are great. Keep a low profile as the climbing is in close proximity to the farm.

1. Jiggle Of The Sphinx
2. Bat Buttress
3. Low Roof

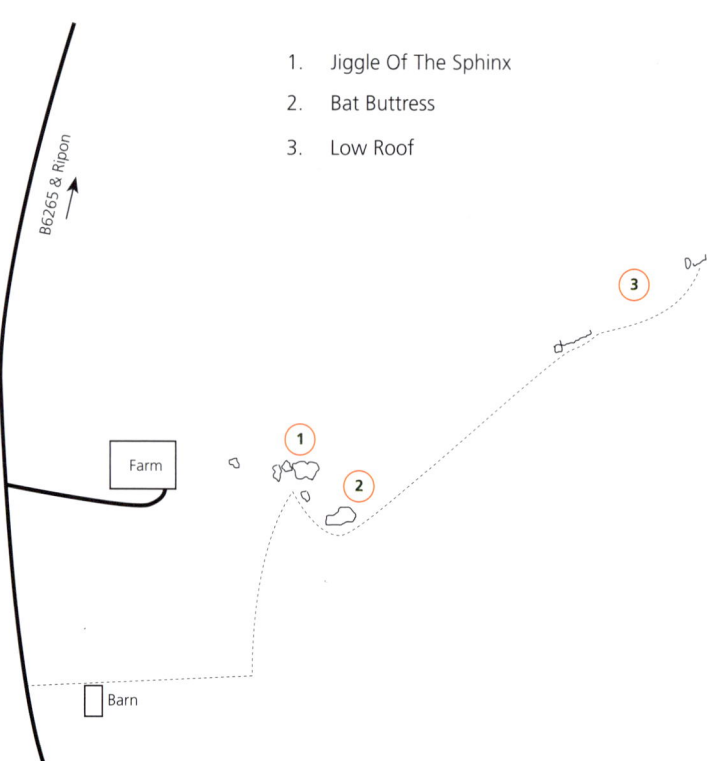

Area 1: Jiggle Of The Sphinx

Area 2: Bat Buttress

1. ● (6a+) **Jiggle Of The Sphinx**
   The reachy arete climbed on the right side.

2. ● (6a)
   The wall next to the arete on unhelpful holds.

About 30m left of the main buttress is a triangular overhanging wall with a hard problem going up the centre and using a block. Vlad Von Carson is around 7c. Starting in the same place but using the left arete is Count Duckula 7a+.

1. ● (5+)
   Tricky left side of the arete.

2. ● (3+)
   Easy ramp up to the flake.

3. ● (4)
   The wall passing slopey breaks.

4. ● (5)
   The arete climbed on the left.

5. ● (6b+) **Riddler**
   The reachy arete climbed on the right side.

6. ● (4) **Bunty**
   Climb the flake leftwards.

7. ● (5) **The Buns Of Naverone**
   Direct version of problem 6. Carry on up the thin flake.

8. ● (6a) **All Buns Blazing**
   The centre of the wall from the undercut. Finishing right on slopers is 6b.

www.aireclothing.com

Area 2: Bat Buttress

1. 🟡 (6a) **Bun Fight At The Ok Corral**
   The blunt arete passing the break.

2. 🟡 (6a+) **The Bun Forgiven**
   Into the seam and finish up the black wall direct.

3. 🔴 (7c)
   The black wall climbed direct via some pebble pulling.

Area 3: Low Roof

1. ● (4)
   The undercut arete.

2. ● (6c)
   SDS. From slopey holds move into the scoop and finish up the vague arete.

3. ● (6a)
   SDS. The right side of the shallow scoop.

4. ● (6a+)
   SDS. Above the block climb into the short corner and finish on the break.

5. ● (6a+)
   SDS. From low flake move up and left passing more flakes.

6. ● (6b)
   SDS. Slopers on the lip, up and over the roof passing poor flakes.

7. ● (6b+)
   SDS. Hard move off pinch up to flat holds through roof.

8. ● (6c+)
   SDS. From the hole in the crack climb direct via a nasty flake.

9. ● (6c+)
   SDS. From the cave/niche move up to a jug and throw for good hold.

10. ● (7a+)
    SDS. Link problem 9 with a low leftwards traverse (feet above plinth) to finish up problem 7.

11. ● (6c+) **Long Good Friday**
    Start as for problem 9 traverse leftwards (feet on plinth) all the way to finish on the crack. Extending the traverse by starting on the right arete is 7b.

12. ● (6b+)
    SDS. The wall climbed leftwards passing open pocket/scoop.

1. ● (4+)
   The highball arete. Possible to escape from break.

2. ● (3+)
   Technical wall left of the crack.

3. ● (3)
   Juggy crack.

4. ● (3)
   The good flake. Finish left of the tree.

Little Brimham/Bovine Buttress

This area offers a number of quality problems in a quiet setting away from the tourists of the main crag. The majority of the quality problems take striking aretes or sharp prow features. Another not so pleasant feature of this area is the nature of the landings which tend to be poor, even with pads the climbing tends to feel committing. This is coupled with the fact that most of the best problems are quite high and require a confident approach. Overall its certainly worth a visit with problems such as Boris Or Bust 6c being one of the best problems of its grade in Yorkshire. Bovine Butress is much more friendly with a number of excellent problems on superb rock and with the added benefit of good landings.

Approach and Access

From the main Brimham car park continue down the road to a public footpath sign opposite the entrance to the farm. The climbing becomes immediately obvious on the right with the classic So Pussy 7b soon coming into view. Please don't walk across the top of the crag to reach Bovine Buttress as you can easily skirt around the bottom of the crag and pick up a good path that contours around to the buttress.

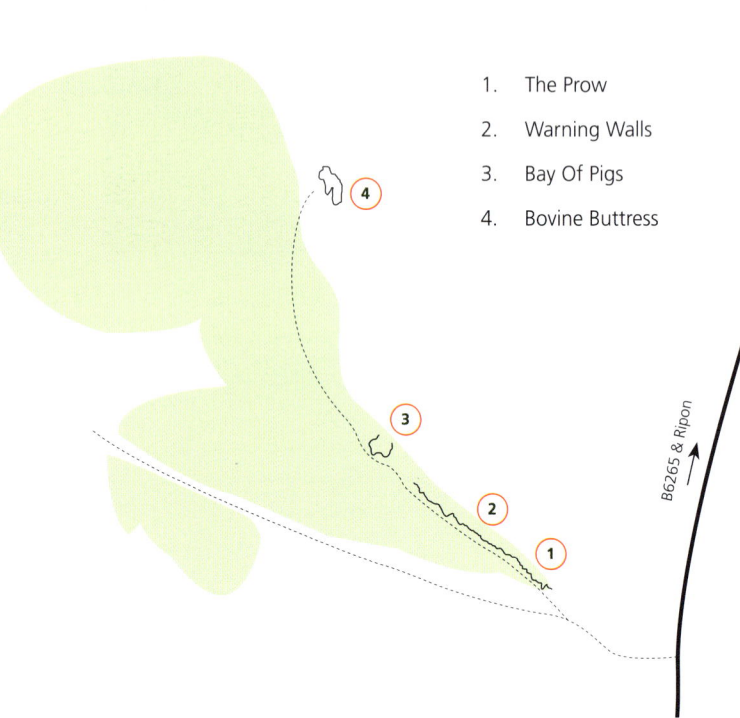

1. The Prow
2. Warning Walls
3. Bay Of Pigs
4. Bovine Buttress

Area 1: The Prow

Area 2: Warning Walls

1. ● (4+) **Thunderball**
The wall passing the shallow runnel.

2. ● (7b) **So Pussy**
SDS. The sandy prow climbed direct.

3. ● (6a) **License To Kill**
From the boulder step on and make a wild throw for the top.

1. ● (4) **Coldfinger**
The crack trending left.

2. ● (4) **On Her Majesty's Secret Service**
The direct into the scoop.

3. ● (6a+) **For Queen And Country**
The prow climbed direct. Highball.

4. ● (6a) **Shaken Not Stirred**
The wall right of the prow passing a flake near the top.

5. ● (6a+) **M**
The right-most line on the wall.

6. ● (6a+) **Live And Let Die**
The often green and dirty rib.

7. ● (6a+) **You Only Live Twice**
The narrow tower.

Area 2: Warning Walls

Area 3: Bay Of Pigs

1. 🟡 (6a) **Bold Finger**
   The often green arete.

2. 🔵 (5+) **Pussy Galore**
   The rib starting on the right.

3. 🟡 (6b) **License To Thrill**
   The slab on slopey holds.

4. 🔵 (5+) **Natasha's Just Deserts**
   The prow climbed on the left side.

5. 🟡 (6c) **Boris Or Bust**
   The terrifying sharp arete.

6. 🔵 (5) **For Your Arms only**
   The wall just right of the prow.

1. 🔴 (7b)
   Highball technical wall with the crux way up above a bad landing.

2. 🟡 (6b+) **Western Alliance**
   SDS. Jugs up into the groove.

3. 🔵 (4) **Supreme Soviet**
   The left edge of the block.

The big arete is excellent but fully E6 due to the terrible landing.

Area 4: Bovine Buttress

1. 🔵 (5+) **The Watering Hole**
   The big wall passing the pocket.
2. 🟡 (6b+) **Cowboy Daze**
   The left side of the undercut arete.
3. 🔵 (5) **Braised Steak**
   From the boulder climb the right side of the nose.
4. 🔵 (5) **Stirk**
   SDS. Undercut wall using the crack and arete.
5. 🔵 (5) **Steer**
   SDS. Undercut wall on the right passing the crack.

1. 🔵 (5+) **Rawhide**
   Gain the highball prow from the crack.
2. 🔵 (5) **Home On The Range**
   Highball wall left of the niche.
3. 🔵 (5) **Just Grazing**
   The left side of the wall passing rough pockets.
4. 🟡 (6c+) **Hang 'em Low**
   L-R traverse across the wall to the break. Finish up the undercut arete.
5. 🔵 (5+) **Riding Bareback**
   The wall on rough holds.
6. 🔴 (7b+)
   Eliminate dyno. From the break throw for the top.
7. 🟡 (6b) **Saddlesore**
   From the left side of the break climb the wall passing the big slopey pocket.
8. 🔵 (5+) **Pony Express**
   The undercut blunt prow.

Crag X

The crag is clearly visible from the road and from a distance it promises to offer lots of bouldering potential. Unfortunately on closer inspection much of the rock is unappealing and offers little scope for quality bouldering. However, all is not lost as a small collection of boulders at the right-hand end of the crag offer excellent problems on superb quality rock. The collection of boulders offers a couple of delightful short aretes as well as a number of hard problems up to 7c+.

Approach and Access
Access is not currently permitted.

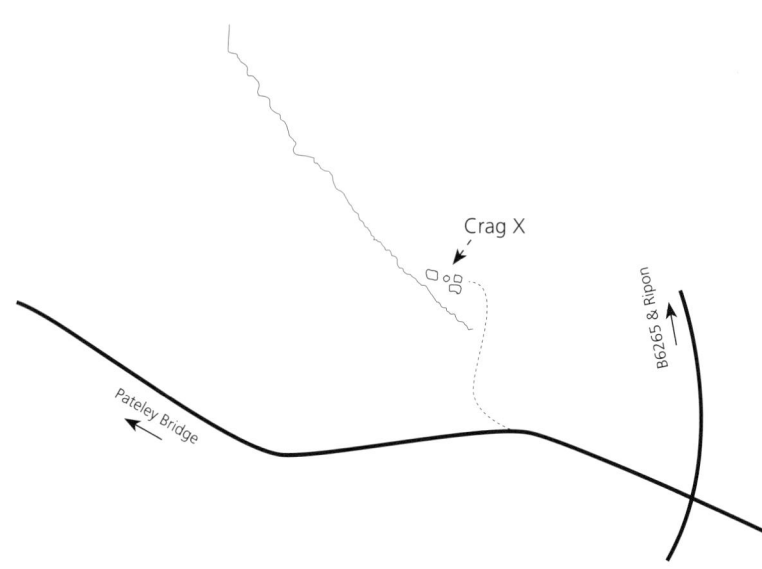

Area 1: Big Fish Boulder

1. ● **(7b) I'm Chief Kamanawanalaya**
SDS. From the low break on the left move rightwards on a thin break to gain the vertical crack. Finish passing the slopey break.

2. ● **(7c+) Big Fish**
SDS. From the thin break climb the blunt arete passing small egdes and slopers. The standing start is 6c.

3. ● **(6b+)**
SDS. From the good flakes make a big stretch to sloper and the top.

4. ● **(7b+)**
SDS. Traverse R-L on the thin break under the small overlap to a finish above the good finger jugs on the left.

1. ● **(5+)**
The pleasant arete can be tackled on either side.

2. ● **(6b+)**
SDS. The clean-cut arete is climbed on the left-hand side.

Fluide

Small but not insignificant area hidden away below the main Brimham areas. This buttress is home to a fantastic problem 'Fluide' 7c courtesy of Yorkshire activist Jim Purchon as well as a superb 6c arete problem as well as the brutal 'Half A Drainpipe' 7b.

Approach and Access

From the main Brimham car park continue down the road passing Maud's Farm until you reach the junction. Cross the junction and after about 50m park considerately next to a public footpath sign. Follow the path to a dry stone wall and cross the wall without damaging it (one part of the wall is very low and can be crossed without touching the wall.) Follow the tree line for 50m before dropping down the hillside to the rocks.

Access is not currently permitted. Check the latest access situation with the BMC.

N.G.R SE206632

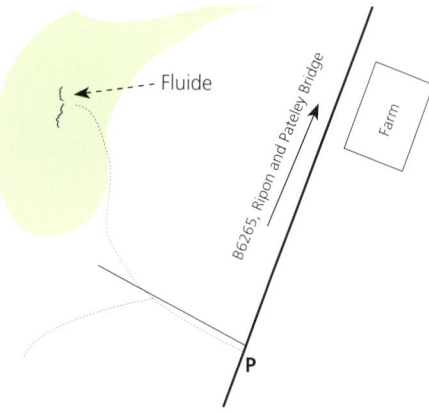

Area 1: Fluide

1. 🟡 (6a)
The technical, clean-cut arete is a superb feature.

2. 🔴 (7c) **Fluide**
The disapearing vertical cracks lead to a undercling and a big move for the top.

3. 🔵 (5+)
The right arete requires good footwork.

1. 🔴 (7b) **Drainpipe**
The superb looking prow is tackled form a standing start.

2. 🟡 (6b+) **After Thought**
The smooth slab is climbed direct passing poor smears.

CALEY ROADSIDE

Toby warming up in the Playground area: Simon Richardson

Caley Roadside

Caley is a world-class bouldering venue with excellent problems throughout the grade range. The bouldering is extremely varied with technical slabs sitting next to mighty highballs as well as more physical testpieces. The volume of problems on offer will keep most climbers busy for a lifetime. The crag faces north, good conditions are enjoyed in both spring and autumn although summer evenings can also offer good friction. The introduction of crash pads has resulted in many of the old micro-routes morphing into modern highballs. Modern classics such as High Fidelity 8b, Zoo York 8a, Terry 7c and the sit-start to Ben's Groove 7c+, sit alongside superb problems such as New Jerusalem 7a, Forked Lightning Crack 6b and Ron's Reach 6a.

Approach and Access

The crag is situated above the A660 Leeds to Otley road just past Pool Bank. Parking is available on the narrow lay-by just below the crag which is easily visible from the road. From here you can access the crag by either the stile at the top of the parking area or via the gate further down the road. The parking is not without its hazards as the lay-by/verge is very narrow and cars flying down the road can come very close to opening doors. Also, when parking you need to access the lay-by, by going down the hill and under no circumstances try and perform a turn in the road when leaving. Two points of access exist for the roadside crag. For the areas Not My Stile and Death Drop, walk back up the road and cross the stile at the top of the lay-by. For the majority of the more central areas cross over the stile just pass the gate at the bottom of the lay-by. Don't climb over the wall.

N.G.R. SE 225445

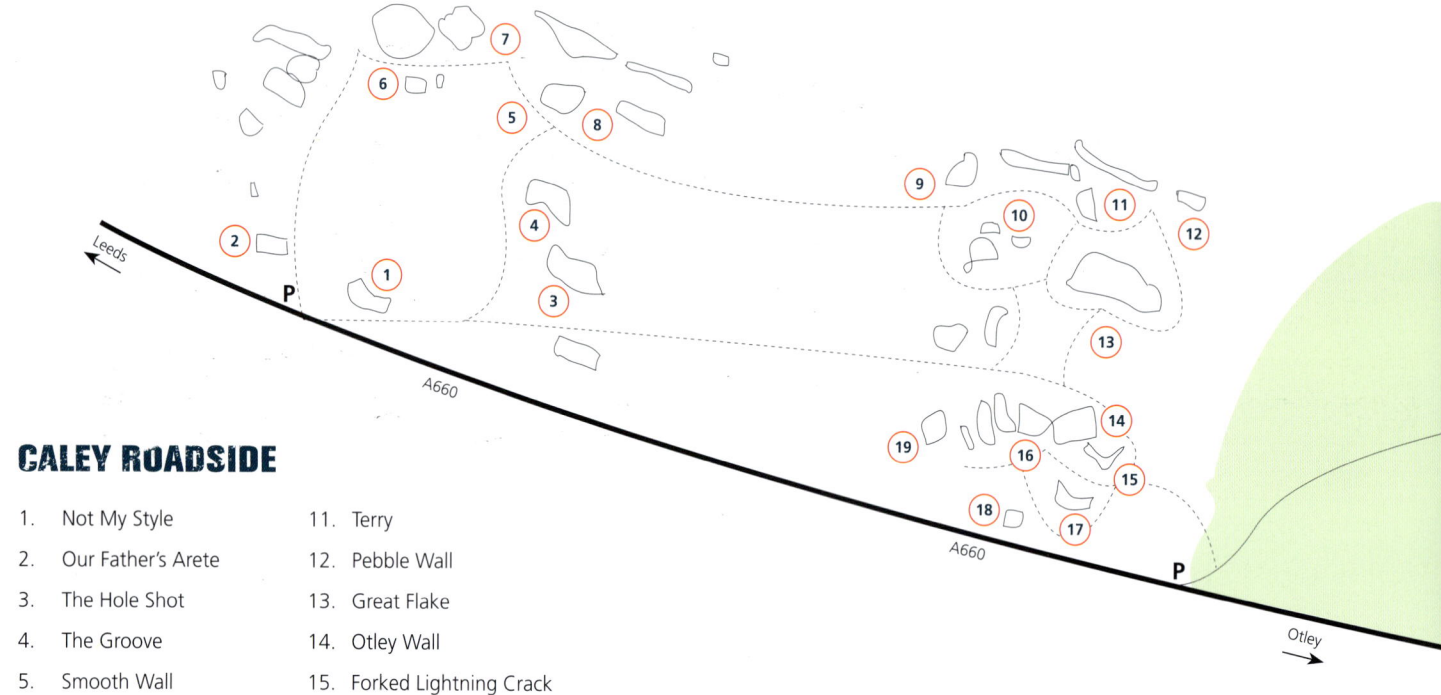

CALEY ROADSIDE

1. Not My Style
2. Our Father's Arete
3. The Hole Shot
4. The Groove
5. Smooth Wall
6. To Be Is Not To Bolt
7. Mini Mati
8. Feel The Noise
9. Blockbuster
10. Ron's Reach
11. Terry
12. Pebble Wall
13. Great Flake
14. Otley Wall
15. Forked Lightning Crack
16. Rabbit Paw Wall
17. No Pebble Arete
18. Roadside Wall
19. The Scoop

Area 1: Not My Style

Area 2: Our Father's Arete

1. ● (6a) **Style Council**
   The small arete.

2. ● (6b+) **Not My Style**
   Left side of rounded arete.

3. ● (4) **Free Style**
   The arete on the right-hand side.

1. ● (5+)
   Crimpy wall left of the arete. SDS. 6a.

2. ● (6a+) **Our Father's Arete**
   The prominent technical arete. SDS. Linking in from problem 1 makes it slightly harder at 6b.

Area 3: The Hole Shot

1. ● (6a)
   From standing start with holds on the lip footless up the arete leftwards.

2. ● (6c) **The Hole Shot**
   From the lip make a blind slap into a hidden crack and finish above.

3. ● (6b+)
   SDS. Desperate mantle via pocket.

4. ● (8b) **Ullola**
   Start standing on short slab before dropping onto the slopey ledge and traversing left to finish up problem 1.

Area 4: The Groove

1. ● (5+)
   SDS. Tough mantle.

2. ● (4)
   Easy slab.

3. ● (5+)
   Follow the runnels to a tricky mantle.

4. ● (5+) **Rough Rib**
   Rounded arete, slightly harder climbed on the right.

5. ● (5+)
   Either span to both aretes or use good slopers.

6. ● (6c+) **The Groove**
   Pad up the groove before making a hard move out right to finish.

7. ● (6c)
   Thin wall left of the arete.

8. ● (5+) **Steady arete**
   Good holds up the right arete.

Area 5: Smooth Wall

1. 🔵 (4+)
   SDS. Finish up the arete.

2. 🟡 (6b+) **Smooth Wall Traverse**
   SDS. Traverse right along break to finish up problem 4.

3. 🔴 (7a+) **Smooth Wall Dyno**
   Big dyno starting just right of the arete.

4. 🟡 (6b) **Smooth Wall**
   The steep wall passing the flake.

5. 🟡 (6c)
   Step on using the undercut and slap for the top.

1. 🟡 (6a+)
   Traverse L-R finishing up the arete.

2. 🟡 (6b+)
   SDS. Slap up to the lip, traverse left to a tricky mantle up the blunt nose.

1. 🔴 (7b) **Just The One**
   Use mono and pinch to slap for the top.

Area 6: To Be Is Not To Bolt

Area 7: Mini Mati

1. 🟡 **(6c+) Death Drop 2000**
   Starting with a stiff pull to some slopers, gain the crack direct.

2. 🔴 **(7c)**
   Desperately thin low-level traverse around the arete to finish up problem 6.

3. 🔴 **(7b) True Pebble Wall**
   Climb the rippled wall just left of the blunt arete. Move left and finish via the runnel.

4. 🔴 **(7b+) Bring Out The Funk**
   Small pebbles give access to the obvious water runnel. E6?

5. 🔴 **(7b) To Be Is Not To Bolt**
   The classic arete with a tricky move high up.

6. 🟡 **(6b) Webster's Whinge**
   Gain the flake and continue up to a usually damp finish.

1. 🟡 **(6b) Martin's Muff**
   The wall via the small flake. Harder and better if you gain the knobble direct.

2. 🟡 **(6b)**
   The line of flakes finishing up to the right.

3. 🔵 **(5+)**
   The arete from a low start on the left.

4. 🔵 **(4+)**
   Climb the short wall.

5. 🔴 **(7b+) Mini Mati**
   The hanging groove above the break. Often wet and seldomly repeated.

Area 8: Feel The Noise

1. 🟡 (6c)
   Start hanging the ledge and make a desperate rock-over into the groove.

2. 🔴 (7C+) **Feel The Noise**
   SDS. From the jug under the roof surmount the lip via small flakes and clusters of pebbles. Standing start is worthwhile at 6c+.

3. 🔴 (7a+) **Ahab**
   The bulge to the right on nasty clusters of pebbles.

1. 🟡 (6c) **Fug Dup**
   SDS. Climb the small but thuggy roof crack.

2. 🔴 (7b+)
   SDS. Starting as low as you can make a couple of powerful slaps out to the lip.

Ben Moon on Ben's Groove: Alex Messenger

Area 9: Blockbuster

1. ● **(7b-7c) Blockbuster**
Grade depends on method. The lower you start the harder it gets. Jump start is 7b.

2. ● **(7c+) Northern Soul**
SDS. The sitter to Blockbuster. Starting in the crack move right to the pocket and pinch, cut loose and join the stand up.

1. ● **(8a) Zoo York** ✱
SDS. Starting on the lowest undercuts. One of the best problems of its grade.

2. ● **(7c+) Guacamola**
Crouching start on good edges. Rock-up to poor crimp and throw for the top. SDS. Start as for Zoo York, move right on undercuts to join problem 2. 8a.

3. ● **(7b+) Ju Ju Club**
SDS. The overhanging groove with a tricky top-out.

Area 10: Ron's Reach

1. ● (7b) **Ripper Arete**
   SDS. The technical arete starting on the left.

2. ● (6a) **Ripper Traverse/Ron's Reach**
   Delicate traverse right to a highball finish.

3. ● (7c) **Freak Technique**
   Mantle onto the slab via the flake. Climb the wall above direct, passing a poor mono.

4. ● (7b+) **Wainright's Wobble**
   Seldomly repeated technical horror. Rock-over onto the slab using pebbles.

5. ● (7b) **Ben's Groove** *
   The standing start is a quality problem with a precarious finish. SDS. One of the best at its grade. 7c+.

6. ● (7b+) **Secret Seventh** *
   Condition dependant arete requiring crafty footwork.

1. ● (5+) **Breakfest**
   SDS. Follow the juggy breaks before finishing up the arete.

Area 10: Ron's Reach

1. 🔵 (4)
   The groove at the left side of the slab.
2. 🔵 (4+)
   The curving groove.
3. 🟡 (6a)
   The vague cracks up the centre of the slab.
4. 🟡 (6a)
   The big, clean-cut arete, climbed on the left-hand side. The right side of the arete is better and harder at 6b+.
5. 🟡 (6b+)
   The crimpy, steep wall with a big lock for the top.
6. 🟡 (6a)
   From the block follow the flake to the crack.

1. 🔵 (5)
   SDS. R-L traverse, finishing with a mantle of the vague nose.

1. 🟡 (6a+)
   R-L traverse of the lip. Drop down to the break at the end.

1. 🟡 (6c+)
   SDS. From the groove, use slopey holds to rock-over onto the slab and finish direct.
2. 🔵 (5+)
   The pleasant groove.

Area 11: Terry

Area 12: Pebble Wall

1. ● (7c) **Terry** ✱
   The perfect grit slab/wall. Low in the grade but hard moves high up make it a big tick. **Gripping Groove** 6a is the technical scoop, left of the wall.

2. ● (7c)
   The wall just left of Syrett's Saunter is super thin and technical.

3. ● (7b) **Syrret's Saunter**
   Brutal pebble pulling up the centre of the slab. Harder, now that a hold has fallen off.

4. ● (6c)
   The left arete of MBKC groove.

5. ● (5+) **MBKC Corner**
   The groove passing a small pocket.

1. ● (6b)
   SDS. Use a pinch to gain the undercut and move right to finish.

2. ● (6a)
   The wall passing a flake. Climbing the groove just to the right is 6b+.

3. ● (5+)
   SDS. From the big ledge rock-up using the arete.

4. ● (7a+)
   SDS. From the flat hold, use holds right of the arete and slap for the top.

Area 13: Great Flake

1. ● (7b+)
   SDS. Tricky moves up to a press hold and a hard slap out left to finish.

2. ● (7b) **Monsoon Monsoon**
   Follow the flake line rightwards to a tricky top-out.

3. ● (7c) **Andy's Wall**
   SDS Sharp undercuts to start gain the scoops on the lip. Then make some worrying moves up and left to a high top-out.

4. ● (7b) **The Great Flake (E6)**
   More route than highball. The sitter to the top of the first flake is worthwhile at 6a.

5. ● (8b) **High Fidelity** ✱
   The awesome arete.

6. ● (7c) **Nothings Safe**
   Superb highball. From break step left and use tiny edges to gain pockets and the slopey top.

Area 14: Otley Wall

Lots of easy warm ups and eliminates exist here.

1. 🔵 (5+) **Courser Edge**
   The arete climbed on its left-hand side.

2. 🔵 (5)
   L-R traverse of the slab with hands below the top.

3. 🟡 (6b+) **Stretcher**
   The wall passing two large rounded pockets. Terrible landing.

4. 🔵 (5+) **Chicken Heads**
   Technical gem.

1. 🔴 (7a+) **Hanging Wall**
   The wall left of the chipped edges trending leftwards.

2. 🔵 (4+) **Chips**
   The chipped edges in the hanging groove. Avoiding chips is 6a+.

3. 🟡 (6b) **Otley Wall Traverse**
   Delicate L-R traverse of the slab starting up problem 1 and finishing up the right arete.

4. 🟡 (6a) **Otley Wall** ★
   Start on the left before stepping right on smears and make a tricky move into the crack.

5. 🔴 (7b+) **Otley Wall Direct**
   Hard rockover into problem 4 using poor dish and pebble.

6. 🟡 (6a)
   The slab starting on the obvious boss.

7. 🔵 (5+) **Courser Edge**
   The arete climbed on its left-hand side.

Area 15: Forked Lightning Crack

1. ● (Easy) **Morris Minor**
   The Chipped slab left of the crack.

2. ● (Easy) **Morris crack**

3. ● (4+) **Morris Dance**
   The wall.

4. ● (6a+) **Maurice Chevalier**
   The left arete climbed on the right-hand side. Use a crimp around the corner. Direct 7a+.

5. ● (?)
   The highball wall right of the arete.

6. ● (6b) **Forked Lightning Crack** ✱
   The awkward curving crack. Traversing in from the left arete is 6c. SDS. 6c.

Tim Stubley at Caley: James Ibbertson

Area 16: Rabbit Paw Wall

1. 🔵 (5+) **Permutation Rib**
   Starting around the corner traversing into the superb arete.

2. 🟡 (6b+) **Permutation Direct**
   From the block climb the arete direct.

3. 🔴 (7c) **Waite**
   Intense bottomless groove from a standing start.

4. 🔵 (4+) **Rabbit Paw Wall**
   The big juggy wall.

1. 🟡 (6b+)
   SDS. Traverse the lip from L-R. Mantle at the apex.

2. 🔴 (7a)
   Dynamic problem using the pocket and edge.

3. 🔴 (7b+) **Crystal Method**
   From the large juggy hold move up to edges and make a shouldery move to gain the top.

4. 🟢 (8a) **Vicious Streak**
   SDS. The right arete via lots of slapping and hugging.

5. 🟡 (6B+)
   The slab right of the rounded arete.

6. 🔴 (7a+)
   Just round the corner, left of the arete of Psycho is a nice dyno.

James Ibbertson on Crystal Method: Tim Stubley

CALEY CRAG

James Ibbertson on One Man And His Dogmas: Adam Long

Caley Crag

Caley Crag is situated just ten minutes walk from the Roadside boulders yet the two crags are very different in character. This crag appears far bigger with some of the buttresses reaching over 15 metres in height and in many respects the problems are more varied. Problems on the larger buttresses follow thin, fingery lines requiring strong fingers and good skin. The boulders scattered below the main buttresses are well-weathered and offer a good selection of rounded problems to work the arms as well as some technical problems which require good foot-work. Another attribute of the crag is that it dries more quickly than the Roadside, although after prolonged rain it can become rather green. During the summer months the Main Crag remains popular due to its lack of bracken cover as well as its northerly aspect.

Approach and Access
Park as for Caley Roadside. Follow the path from Caley gate for 400m keeping to the main path. The first boulder reached is the large chipped face of 'Suckers Wall.'

N.G.R. SE 225445

CALEY CRAG

1. Suckers Wall
2. Smear Arete
3. Boot Crack
4. Low Traverse
5. Banana Republic
6. Roof Of The World
7. Pedestal Arete
8. Juha's Arete
9. Tombstone
10. One Man And His Dogmas
11. Hanging Flake
12. Sugarloaf Buttress
13. The Pancake
14. The Horn
15. The Flapjack
16. The Yule Log
17. Chicken Run
18. The Sandwich
19. The Fairy Cake
20. The Cream Eggs

Area 1: Suckers Wall

1. ● (4+)
   Chipped edges just right of the left arete.

2. ● (5+)
   The middle of the wall up the chipped edges.

3. ● (5+) **Twin Pockets**
   Step off the boulder and climb the wall passing a big pocket. Starting from the ground is 6b+.

4. ● (7b+) **Scary Canary**
   The highball left side of the front face.

5. ● (5+) **Suckers Rib**
   The blunt rib passing lots of chipped holds.

6. ● (4+) **Suckers Wall**
   The line of chipped holds up the centre of the face.

7. ● (7a+) **Front Traverse**
   Traverse the wall from left-right, starting on the far left arete. Finish up Suckers wall.

1. ● (7b+)
   Start up the right-hand side of the arete until a positive hold on the arete allows you to swing around onto the slabby side. Finish direct.

2. ● (8a) **Mistaken Identity**
   Hard direct start into the hanging flake. Starting on the right is 7c+.

3. ● (7b+)
   From the slopey ledge use a poor hold up and left to throw for the top.

4. ● (6b+) **The Pinch**
   The slopey ledge up and right to a good pinch and the top.

CALEY CRAG

117

Area 2: Smear Arete

1. 🟡 (6c)
   SDS. Pockets, sidepull then top.

2. 🔴 (7b)
   SDS. From the undercut gain two edges and throw for the top.

1. 🟡 (6b+)
   Technical wall just left of problem 2.

2. 🔵 (5+) **Smear Arete** ✱
   The left side of the sharp arete. The right side is slightly harder at 6a.

3. 🟡 (6b)
   SDS. L-R traverse pulling over the nose.

Area 2: Smear Arete

1. 🔵 **(5+) Truffle**
   The slab next to the leaning arete.

2. 🔴 **(7a+) The Prow**
   SDS. Clamp up the steep prow. Standing start is 6b+.

3. 🔴 **(7a+)**
   SDS. Crimpy edges into the crack above.

1. 🔴 **(7b+) Point Break**
   SDS. The left side of the roof, avoiding the block.

Area 3: Boot Crack

1. 🟡 **(6b+) Back Wall**
   The wall left of and avoiding the arete.

2. 🟡 **(6b) Pocket Rock**
   The arete on the left side. SDS. 7a.

3. 🟡 **(6b) Back Stabber**
   The crimpy wall just right of the arete.

4. 🟡 **(6c) Rick's Rock** ✷
   The centre of the wall on thin but positive edges. Gets reachy just when you don't want to fall off.

5. 🟡 **(6a) Black Jumper**
   Highball arete with bad landing.

1. 🔴 **(7b)**
   Seldomly repeated highball. Climb the slab until the holds run out. Move onto and finish up the left arete.

2. 🟡 **(6c)**
   R-L traverse. From the crack traverse under the roof avoiding the chipped holds. Finish on the slab.

3. 🟡 **(6a)**
   Stiff pull from under the roof onto the wall. Finish up the arete.

4. 🔵 **(4+) Shoe Shine**
   The highball arete.

5. 🔵 **(5+) Sneakers**
   The big wall climbed just left of centre.

6. 🔵 **(5) Green Streak**
   The right side of the wall.

Area 4: Low Traverse

1. 🟡 (6b)
R-L traverse finishing up the blunt nose.

1. 🔵 (5)
The short arete.

2. 🔵 (5)
SDS. The wall passing the side-pull.

3. 🔵 (5)
SDS. From the arete swing up right onto the wall.

4. 🔵 (5)
SDS. The short hanging arete.

5. 🟡 (6a)
SDS. Surmount the roof from the pocket.

Steve Dunning on Shoe Shine: Pete Chadwick

Area 5: Banana Republic

1. ● (8a) **Banana Republic**
SDS. The right side of the leaning arete. Hard couple of moves off poor edges to get established on the stand up, which is worth 7b+.

Area 6: Roof of The World Area

1. 🟡 (6b)
   The left arete climbed on the steep side.

2. 🔵 (5+) **Roof Of The World**
   Footless up the prow. SDS. Hard pull off the ground into a nasty shoulder press 7c+.

3. 🟡 (6b)
   The right arete climbed on the steep side.

1. 🔵 (5+)
   SDS. Follow the lip to a tricky mantle.

Area 7: Pedestal Arete

Left of problem 1 are a number of problems in the 4-5+ range. Unfortunately these remain out of condition for much of the year and see little, if any attention from the modern boulderer.

1. ● **(6a)**
   From the nose smear up the slab.

2. ● **(7c+) No More Mr Next Try**
   Highball wall. (Hanging rope used on first ascent to pull through the hedge at the top)

3. ● **(7a+) Slapstick arete**
   SDS. The right-hand arête. Start from the large hold down and left.

1. ● **(6a) Forecourt Crawler**
   Climb the crack escaping right.

2. ● **(7a+) Forecourt Traverse**
   From the crack traverse L-R on thin crimps and poor pockets to eventually pull around onto the slab.

3. ● **(7c+) Pedestal Arete**
   SDS. Start on the left-hand side of the arête, right hand on arête and left on a small crimp. Starting on the right or using a heel on the good hold around the arête is 7b+. A standing start is 7a.

4. ● **(6b)**
   The centre of the scooped slab without using the arete.

Area 7: Pedestal Arete

1. ● (5+)
   The easy side of the arete.

2. ● (6a)
   The overhanging side of the arete. The wall without the arete is 6c.

3. ● (4+)
   The slabby side of the clean-cut arete.

4. ● (6a) **Double Rib Traverse**
   Traverse L-R across the slab from arete to arete without using the chipped holds.

5. ● (6b+)
   A thin side-pull moves you onto the committing slab.

6. ● (6a)
   Scooped wall just left of the arete. Finish up the slab.

7. ● (4+)
   The sharp arete. Escape from the ledge.

Suzan Dudink on Pedestal Arete. Darren Stevenson

Area 8: Juha's Arete

1. 🟢 **(8a) Ranieri's Reach**
Quality line from Ben Moon. Starting in the crack move out right onto the thin traverse line. Hard moves on poor edges all the way out to the right arete. Finish up the arete and escape rightwards.

2. 🟠 **(7c) Juha's Arete** *
The blank right arete. Using the arete and an undercling make a dynamic move for the distant pocket. Finish up the arete and escape rightwards.

Ben Moon on Ranieri's Reach: Alex Messenger

Area 9: Tombstone

1. ● (6c)
   The left arete with the poor crack.

2. ● (7a)
   The wall right of the crack without reaching onto the arete.

3. ● (6a) **Fingers Crack**
   Finger-lock your way up the well-worn crack.

4. ● (6b)
   The wall between the crack and the arete without using either.

5. ● (4+) **Epitaph**
   The leaning side of the arete. The slabby side is 3+.

1. ● (6b+)
   The left arête is tackled on its steeper side. The slabby side is much easier at 4+.

2. ● (4+)
   The centre of the block passing the flake.

3. ● (5)
   The delicate right arete of the block.

4. ● (3+)
   The left arete of the large boulder just next to the cleft.

5. ● (5)
   The middle of the big slab passing a flake and finishing direct.

6. ● (4+)
   The delicate right arete of the block. Avoiding the chips makes it 5.

Area 10: One Man And His Dogmas

1. 🔴 **(7b+) One Man And His Dogmas**
   Excellent highball. The landing is not the best. Start on the wall to the left and gain the break then move left to finish up the arete. The direct start is 7c.

2. 🟡 **(6b+)**
   The vague arête is a far less committing challenge but excellent all the same.

1. 🔵 **(4+) Short Arete**
   The left arete.

2. 🔵 **(4+) Rippled Wall**
   The rippled wall is climbed direct.

This is the last boulder described along the edge. The next area described is the collection of large boulders below.

Area 11: Hanging flake

1. 🔴 **(7a+) Dr Green Thumb**
The wall just right of the far left arete (around the corner.) Avoiding holds on the arete.

2. 🔵 **(4+)**
The groove right of the left arete.

3. 🟡 **(6c) Green Wall**
The centre of the highball wall. Dirty.

4. 🟡 **(6a+) Green Wall Arete**
The left-hand side of the arete. The right-hand side is a 5 with poor landing.

1. 🔵 **(5+)**
The steep left side of the wall passing a good flake and a small pocket.

2. 🟡 **(6b) Hanging Flake**
The centre of the wall passing the large hanging flake. Sustained.

As the woodland becomes thicker the boulders become smaller and of less interest. However, if you follow the good track for 50m before dropping down to the right you will stumble upon a fine block which is home to 'Two Squirrels,' a classic 7b+ traverse. Start sitting with both hands in the crack and traverse left to finish up the far left arête. Starting in the same place and finishing up the first arête by some beefy clamping is 'The Drey', a superb but reachy 7c.

Area 12: Sugarloaf Buttress

A little on the high side for bouldering, the Sugarloaf has a number of traverses and the odd nice problem/solo for the brave.

1. ● **(5) Angel's Wall**
   Big pulls between good holds on the lower wall to a heart-fluttering pull around the left side of the triangular roof.

2. ● **(6a) Angel's Wing**
   Starting near the right arete use good spaced holds to reach a junction with problem 1. Avoid the right arete.

The opposite (north) side of the boulder has a number of routes/extended problems. The right-hand rib is Sweet Tooth **4+** and its direct start is **5+**. Right of these is a good warm up problem taking the centre of the wall.

Area 13: The Pancake

1. ● **(6c+)**
   SDS. Stiff couple of pulls from the scoop to get established on the slab.

2. ● **(7a)**
   Hanging start on the pocket, throw for the next one and mantle onto the slab.

3. ● **(6c)**
   SDS. From the sloper use the undercut to a hard press onto the slab.

4. ● **(6a) Mr Smooth**
   Pull onto the slab just left of the blunt arete. Strictly speaking the arete is out at the start but it makes a great problem feel contrived. SDS. **6b**.

Area 14: The Horn

Area 15: The Flapjack

1. ● (7a+)
The left side of the arete on poor slopey holds.

2. ● (6b)
The prow using everything. Frustrating until you suss out the knack.

3. ● (6c)
The right arete of the prow.

1. ● (7a) **Flapjack Traverse**
L-R traverse. Starting on the left arete traverse rightwards with hands below the top, passing the groove to finish along the slab.

2. ● (6c)
SDS. Stiff pull from the flake in the shallow groove with a mantle finish. Hard for the tall. The stand up is 5+.

3. ● (5)
Tricky mantle from the two good crimps.

4. ● (5+)
The slab left of the scoop.

5. ● (5)
The scoop requires good footwork.

6. ● (4)
The easy-angled right arete.

Area 16: The Yule Log

1. 🔴 (7a)
   SDS. Small, nasty edges with a stiff pull into the scoop.

2. 🟡 (6c)
   SDS. Sustained arete climbed on the left-hand side.

3. 🔵 (4)
   Steady slab just right of arete on good nobbles.

1. 🔵 (3+)
   The wall passing the pocket.

2. 🔵 (3+)
   The centre of the slab.

3. 🔵 (5+)
   SDS. Use the undercut to pull onto the slab.

4. 🔵 (3+)
   The undercut flake line.

Area 17: The Chicken Run

Area 18: The Sandwich

1. 🟡 (6b+) **Goose bumps**
   The wall above the plinth.

2. 🟡 (6b+)
   Traverse the block L-R below the top. Finish on the easy side of the block.

3. 🟡 (6a) **Drumstick**
   The arete passing the good flake.

4. 🔴 (7a+) **The Chicken Run**
   The wall without either arete.

5. 🔵 (5+) **Cold Turkey**
   The short but quality arete.

1. 🟡 (6a)
   From the undercut slap up to slopers and rock-over onto the slab.

2. 🔵 (5+)
   Use the undercut and sloper to gain the pocket and rock-over.

3. 🔵 (5+)
   The wall left of the arete. Avoiding the arete.

Area 19: The Fairy Cake

1. 🟡 6a+ **The Scone**
   Traverse the slopers L-R. Starting on the slab and linking onto the slopers is 7a.

2. 🔵 5+
   The slab just right of the arete.

3. 🟡 6a
   The centre of the slab passing vague pockets.

4. 🔵 4+
   The delicate right arete.

Area 20: The Cream Eggs

1. 🟠 7a+ **Over Easy**
   SDS. The undercut arete.

2. 🟡 6c+ **Cream Egg Eliminate**
   From the right arete, smear up leftwards via an undercut, swap hands and use a chicken head to gain the top.

3. 🟠 7b **Scrambled Egg**
   SDS. Link the start of problem 1 into problem 2.

4. 🟡 6a+
   Smear up the right arete.

5. 🟡 6a
   SDS. Climb the tricky left arete.

6. 🟡 6c
   SDS. Climb the wall between the two aretes, passing the break.

7. 🟡 6a
   SDS. Traverse rightwards along the lip and rock-over the nose.

yorkshiregrit

www.yorkshiregrit.com

News • photos • videos • comments • grade votes

EAST & WEST CHEVIN

Steve Dunning on Like A Hurricane: Dalvinder Sodhi

East and West Chevin

Above Caley the Chevin crags stretch westwards in a thick woodland. Both East and West Chevin offer high quality problems, yet neither are particularly extensive. The East Chevin crags have a number of fine problems between 7c and 8a, with plenty of quality warm ups. However, West Chevin has one of the best problems in the area 'Brownian Motion' a very stiff 7c+, along with some worthwhile low grade problems. Both crags face north and would benefit from some traffic.

Approach and Access

For West Chevin approach from Menston. From Bradford Road turn onto Buckle Lane at the traffic lights. Follow this until a right fork picks up Windmill Lane. Turn left at the end of the road before turning immediately right onto York Gate. After approximately 100m a gate can be seen on the left. Park in the lay-by and walk across the field. Turn right immediately upon entering the wood. 5min. East Chevin is approached in minutes from Otley centre via the A660. After leaving the centre of Otley the road follows a steep bank for 500m at which point the car park becomes clear on the right.

N.G.R. SE 213445

EAST & WEST CHEVIN

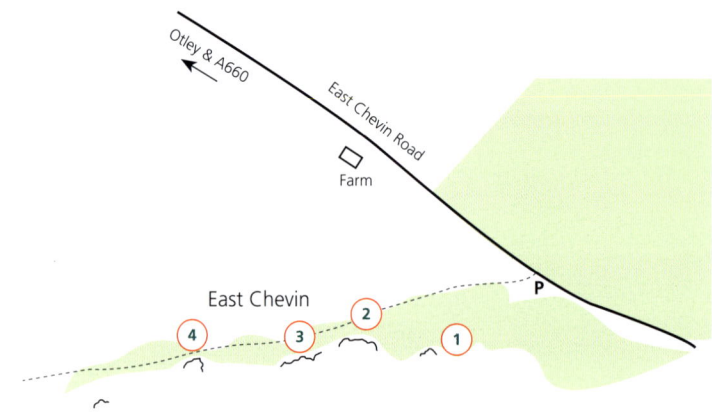

West Chevin

1. West Chevin

East Chevin

1. Harvest
2. Alter Ego
3. Mortal Wall
4. Like A Hurricane

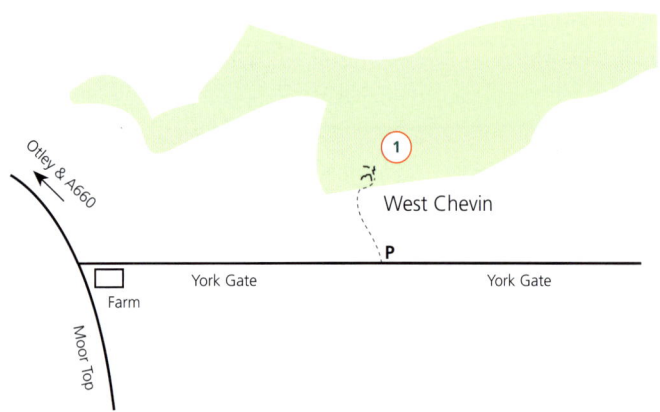

Area 1: Harvest

Area 2: Alter Ego

1. ● (8a) **Harvest**
   SDS. The sharp prow climbed direct. Desperate finish. This boulder is situated on a narrow shelf just above the quarry. A track forks off leftwards at the edge of the quarry and the boulder is visible above.

1. ● (6b) **Alter Ego**
   SDS. The left arete climbed on the left-hand side.

2. ● (6b)
   SDS. The left arete climbed on the right-hand side.

3. ● (6b+)
   SDS. The steep wall on good pockets.

4. ● (6b) **Alter Ego Traverse**
   SDS. Start as for problem 1 traverse right to finish up problem 5.

5. ● (6b+)
   SDS. The pocketed wall.

Area 3: Mortal Wall

Area 4: Like a Hurricane

1. 🔵 **(5+) Mortal Wall**
   The wall via the impressive feature.

1. 🔴 **(7c+) Like A Hurricane**
   SDS. Start at the back of the plinth, slap out to the far arete before making a committing rock-over onto the jug. Finish up the groove.

2. 🟢 **(8a) Omega**
   SDS. Start as for problem 1 until the hanging arete can be tackled on its left side.

Area 1: West Chevin

1. ● (5) **The Barn Door**
The right arete.

2. ● (6a) **Unit Of Power**
Just left of the arete.

3. ● (6a) **Sideliner**
Wall on sidepulls just right of the centre.

4. ● (5+) **Super Central**
The centre of the wall passing a slot.

5. ● (6a) **Blobby**
The wall passing the blobby hold.

6. ● (6a+) **Ground Up**
The scooped wall.

1. (7b) ● **Particle collision**
The highball left arete. More like E4/5!

2. (7c+) ● **Brownian Motion**
The centre of the wall via a poor crimp. Highball classic. Still to be climbed without stretching for the arete.

Area 1: West Chevin

1. 🟡 (6b) **The Green Wing**
   The R-L traverse.

2. 🟡 (6b+) **Missing Time**
   Link problem 1 into problem 3.

3. 🟡 (6a+) **Time**
   Left arete stepping left to finish.

1. 🔵 (4+) **How Green Was My Valley**
   The crack on the right.

2. 🟡 (6a) **Supergreen**
   Just left of the arete.

3. 🟡 (6a+) **Homeland**
   The arete to the ledge with an easy finish.

4. 🟡 (6b+) **Walking The Plank**
   The wall without the arete.

5. 🟡 (6a) **Exorcist Green**
   The left arete.

Area 1: West Chevin

1. 🟡 (6a+) **Defence System**
Thin central crack.

2. 🔵 (5+) **Twin Finish**
The crack on the left.

1. 🔴 (7a+) **Eat The Light**
From the crimps move diagonally leftwards on small edges to a large jug.

2. 🟡 (6b+) **Avatar**
Go up and right from the same starting crimps.

EARL CRAG

Pete Chadwick on Slim Shady: Steve Dunning

Earl Crag

Earl crag is home to some of the finest problems in this guide, standing high above the dark village of Cowling, it is a boulderers' delight. The northerly aspect of the crag ensures that good conditions can be enjoyed in the summer months. It can be bitterly cold in winter but if the wind is not blowing directly onto the cliff it is still climbable. Its exposed aspect means it is quick to dry after rain and often provides great conditions for hard sends.

It was considered a backwater until recent years and the majority of the development has been the work of local devotees. Jerry Peel and Dave Buchanan climbed some of the finest testpieces on Yorkshire grit, these include Dave's Groove 7c and Jerry's Desert Island Arete 7a. Many of Yorkshire's hard-core boulderers made their first exploits to the crag after the plum line of Underworld 7c+ fell to Peak raider Ben Moon in 2000 and since then the crag has remained popular as a venue for the enthusiastic boulderer.

Approach and Access

Clearly visible on the skyline above Cowling on the Keighley-Colne Road (A6068). Take the left turn (Dick Lane) immediately on entering Cowling from Crosshills. The road runs below the crag passing limited parking opportunities just passed the quarry at the far end of the crag. Alternatively, follow the road until you reach a cross-roads and turn right. After about 1/2 mile to the car park is on the right. Take care when accessing the car park as the entrance has large protruding rocks that won't do your car any favours should you bump one. The path leads directly to the Monument Area.

N.G.R. SD 988429

EARL CRAG

1. Erasor Slab
2. Sloping Beauty
3. Desert Island Arete
4. The Flakes
5. The Pinnacle
6. Isolated Pinnacle
7. The Hitching Stone

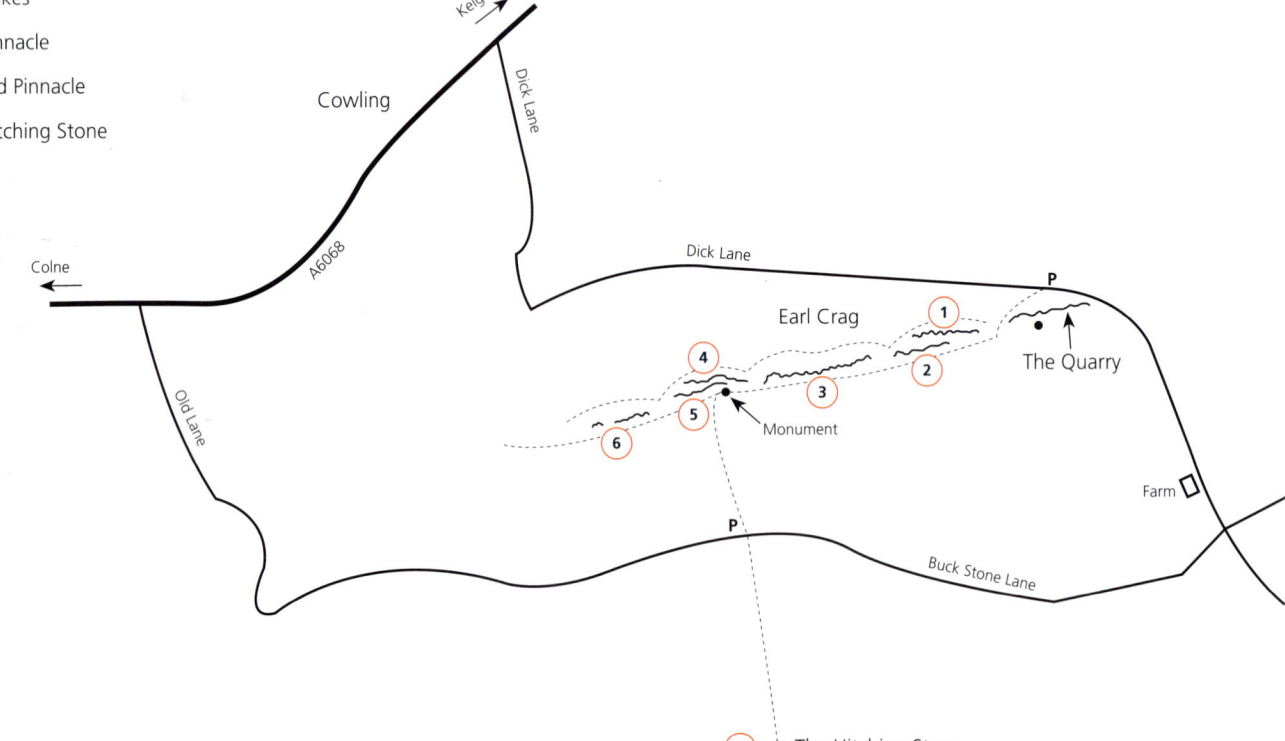

The Quarry

Situated at the far left of Earl Crag a broken quarry gives a number of highball problems. Scope for further additions exist but take care as the landings are far worse than they first appear.

You will notice an excellent overhanging wall in the first bay (entering the quarry from the road) but unfortunately nearly all the holds are manufactured (either drilled or stuck on). This was the work of a group of Lancashire climbers/construction engineers!

1. ● (7c+) **After Dark**
   The technical arch is much harder than it looks.

2. ● (7b) **In Stitches**
   Highball blunt arete.

3. ● (7a) **Sicca**
   The groove into a vague niche finishing up the small ramp.

Area 1: Erasor Slab

1.1 First Boulder
1.2 Hanging Wall
1.3 Problem Wall
1.4 Erasor Slab
1.5 Green Bits
1.6 The Prow

Area 1.1: First Boulder

The very first boulder reached (when approaching from the quarry) is fairly short but it does have a couple of nice problems on a clean arete. Both sides of the arete go at 6a starting from sitting.

Area 1.2: Hanging Wall

Area 1.3: Problem Wall

1. ● (6c)
   SDS. From the right arete rock-up and right to finish.

2. ● (6b)
   Start up the right arete and traverse the lip from right to left.

1. ● (6b)
   Hard undercut wall.

2. ● (6c+)
   The often green arete.

3. ● (6b) **Problem Wall**
   Thin climbing up the centre of the wall.

1. ● (6a) **Pitch At Will**
   The undercut arete of the next boulder is committing.

2. ● (6b)
   Start at an undercut and gain the break by a hard pull, traverse off rightwards.

3. ● (6b+) **Greg's Arete**
   The right arete requires a committed approach.

Area 1.4: Erasor Slab

Area 1.5: Green Bits

1. 🟡 **(6b) Kipper**
   SDS. Escape at the break. Another good problem starts up Kipper, before traversing leftwards, turning the arete and finishing leftwards 6b+.

2. 🔵 **(5+) Eraser Slab**
   Classic highball. Climbing direct is 6a.

3. 🟡 **(6b+)**
   Climb the wall direct.

1. 🔵 **(5) Pedestal Rib**
   From the pedestal climb the steep wall, move right around the arete to finish. Finishing left of the arete is 6a.

2. 🟡 **(6b+)**
   Dynamic problem into the hole in the middle of the wall and link into problem 1.

Area 1.6: The Prow

1. ● (6a) **Lower Indicator**
   SDS. The undercut fin left of the roof.

2. ● (6b+) **Cosmic Baby**
   SDS. Climb the roof direct onto the slab and escape.

3. ● (6b) **Time to Go**
   The wall to the left of the corner.

Ross Gordon at Earl Crag: Steve Dunning

Area 2: Sloping Beauty

2.1 Edge Of Darkness
2.2 Hand Full
2.3 Sloping Beauty
2:4 Undercut Arete
2.5 Trick Arete
2.6 Low Rider
2.7 Cool Hand
2.8 Low Slab

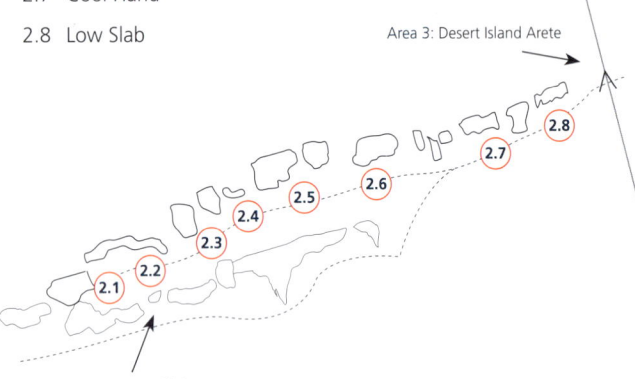

Area 2.1: Edge Of Darkness

1. ● (7c) **Edge Of Darkness** ✶
The crimpy wall on poor pockets to gain the crack, jump off or solo an E5.

2. ● (5+)
Reachy arete climbed on its left-hand side. 6c climbed on its right. Escape into gully from the break.

3. ● (6a) **Rubber Arete** ✶
Tricky arete, escape at the break into the gully.

4. ● (4+) **Rubber Wall**
Good pockets up the easy angled wall.

Area 2.2: Hand Full

Area 2.3: Sloping Beauty

1. 🟡 (6a) **Hand Full Arete**
   Excellent rounded arete, slightly harder if you stick to the right side. Bad landing.

2. 🔵 (5+)
   The wall to the right of the arete.

1. 🟡 (6b) **Hanging Groove** ✱
   SDS. Classic problem.

2. 🔴 (7a)
   Climb problem 1 traverse thin break left and jump for the top. 6B+ from standing.

3. 🟢 (8a) **Vanishing Point**
   The superb arete from standing.

4. 🔴 (7b) **Sloping Beauty** ✱
   The wall via a pocket and a sloper. Dynamic.

5. 🔴 (7b) **Sutty's Dyno**
   From the fat undercuts jump for the top. Bad landing.

6. 🟡 (6b)
   Climb the roof onto the slab via the obvious seam.

Area 2.4: Undercut Arete

1. 🟡 (6b) **Undercut Arete**
   SDS. Small arete is harder than it looks. Thuggy.

Area 2.5: Trick Arete

1. 🔵 (4+)
   The centre of the wall and capping roof. Highball.

2. 🟡 (6b) **Trick Arete**
   Classic Earl Crag sandbag.

3. 🟡 (6b)
   The wall right of Trick Arete.

4. 🟡 (6c)
   The super thin wall.

Area 2.6: Low Rider

1. 🟡 (6a)
   SDS. Traverse left from the scoop to finish up the blunt arete via the slot.

2. 🔵 (5+)
   SDS. As for problem 1 but finish direct from slot.

3. 🟡 (6b)
   SDS. From the jug slap for the top.

4. 🟡 (6b)
   SDS. The steep arete.

5. 🟡 (6c)
   R-L traverse of the lip starting in the crack and finishing as for problem 1.

Area 2.7: Cool Hand

1. 🔵 (5+) **Cool Hand Wall**
   Centre of the wall.
   6a start hanging break.

2. 🟡 (6a) **Cool Hand**
   The technical arete.

3. 🔵 (5+)
   The groove via the slot.

Area 2.8: Low Slab

Just below the main edge is a pleasant boulder with a number of technical problems on a pebbly slab and a couple on a steeper face. The boulder is close to the wall and faces the road.

1. 🟡 (6a+) **Centre Court**
   The middle of the slab on sharp pebbles and poor pockets.

2. 🔵 (4+)
   Slab next to the arete.

3. 🟡 (6b+)
   SDS. The arete climbed on the steep side.

4. 🟡 (6b+)
   SDS. The wall via flakes.

5. 🟡 (6b)
   SDS. The right arete.

Area 3: Desert Island Arete

3.1 Simple Arete
3.2 Butterfly Wall
3.3 Konrad Bartelski
3.4 Desert Island Arete
3.5 Rat Au Van
3.6 Sour Grapes
3.7 Grape Nut
3.8 Handy Andy's

Area 3.1: Simple Arete

1. 🟡 (6a) **Simple Arete**
Clean arete.

2. 🔵 (5+) **Simple Slab**
Slab right of the arete.

3. 🔵 (5+)
Short arete.

4. 🟡 (6b+) **Ribber**
The wall via pockets.

Area 3.2: Butterfly Wall

1. 🟡 (6b) **Green Rib**
   The arete and wall climbed on its right. **Prime Rib** finishes by traversing the break into the groove 6b+.

2. 🟡 (6B+) **Green Rib Right-Hand**

3. 🔴 (7c+) **Slim Shady**
   Start left hand pinch, right hand on the crimp. Escape at the break.

4. 🔴 (7a) **Butterfly Wall**
   Often green. Escape from the break..

5. 🔴 (7b) **Superfly**
   Arete with monos.

Photo: Alex Messenger

Area 3.3: Konrad Bartelski

Area 3.4: Desert Island Arete

1. 🟡 **(6b+) Konrad Bartelski**
   Climb the overhanging jammed block.

2. 🟡 **(6b) The Way Home**
   Arete from SDS.

3. 🟡 **(6B) Long Way Home**
   L-R traverse finish up Mow Wall.

4. 🟡 **(6c)**
   Hard moves up the steep wall left of the arete.

5. 🟡 **(6a+) Mow Wall**
   The wall passing the slot.

1. 🟡 **(6c+) Desert Island Arete** ★
   SDS. Links in from the jug under the roof at 7b. Escape at the break.

2. 🔴 **(7b) Dave's Start**
   SDS. Link into Desert Island Arete from the slot.

3. 🔴 **(7b) Andy's Problem**
   Climb the right side of the arete finishing up the vague rib. SDS. 7b+. Escape at the break.

Area 3.5: Rat Au Van

Area 3.6: Sour Grapes

1. 🔵 (5+)
   The Rib.

2. 🟡 (6a)
   Undercut arete.

3. 🟡 (6a) **Rat Au Van**
   Clean arete.

4. 🔵 (4+)
   Lay-back the crack.

5. 🟡 (6c)
   The wall right of the corner is good when clean.

1. 🟡 (6b) **Sour Grapes Traverse**
   Traverse L-R along the break at the back of the roof.

Area 3.7: Grape Nut

Area 3.8: Handy Andy's

1. ● (6c) **The Boundary**
   The groove next to the wall.

2. ● (7a+) **Grape Nut** ✱
   Tough getting off the floor but it ain't over until it's over. SDS. 7c.

3. ● (7c) **Krafty**
   The undercut left arete with less than ideal landing.

4. ● (6a)
   The blunt, undercut arete right of the block. No sneaking off right.

1. ● (5)
   The left-most blunt arete.

2. ● (5+)
   Slabby wall right of the arete.

3. ● (4+)
   The steep side of the arete.

4. ● (5+) **Iggy's Groove**
   The right wall of the corner passing a pocket.

5. ● (5+)
   The right arete of the corner. SDS. 6c.

6. ● (7a) **Handy Andy's**
   Starting on the ledge step onto the overhanging face. Standing start 7c.

7. ● (5+)
   The left arete climbed on the right-hand side.

8. ● (7b) **Andy Brown's Wall**
   The middle of the wall, dyno for the top.

Area 4: The Flakes

4.1 The Flakes
4.2 The John Dunne Slap
4.3 Down Under
4.4 Australia Roof

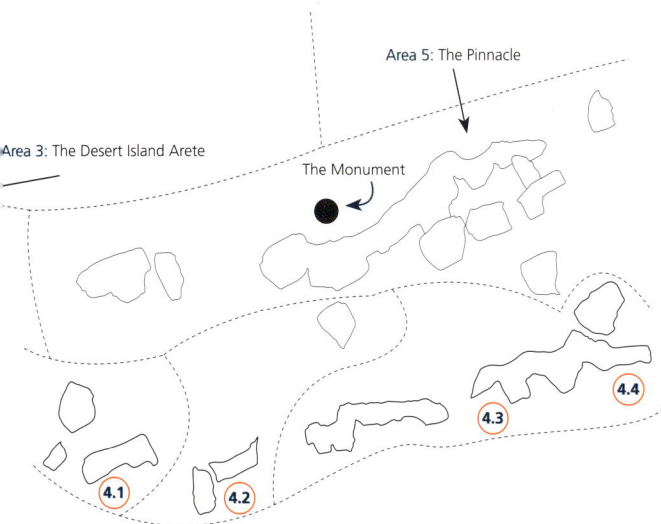

Area 4.1: The Flakes

1. 🟡 (6b+)
   The reachy wall passing a poor crimp.

2. 🟡 (6c) **The gimp**
   Climbed on the left. 7b+ starting and finishing on the right.

3. 🟠 (7b) **The Flakes**
   Start up the ramp before breaking out left to edge then top.

4. 🟠 (7c) **Dave's Groove** ✲
   Classic problem, one of the best 7c problems on grit. 7c+ from a sitter.

5. 🟢 (8a+) **Twelve Bore**
   Poor lay-aways make for a hard step-on, dynamic finish.

Steve Dunning on Grape Nut: Alex Messenger

Area 4.2: The John Dunne Slap

1. 🟡 **(6c) Ron's Slab**
   The centre of the big slab.

2. 🟡 **(6c) Ron's Arete** ✶
   Move left at the top.

3. 🟡 **(6b+) The John Dunne Slap**
   Classic dynamic problem. Done static at similar grade.

Area 4.3: Down Under

Area 4.4: Australia Roof

1. 🔴 **(7a+) Down Under**
   The twin ribs right of the arete have a bad landing and the grade is unconfirmed.

2. 🟡 **(6a)**
   The high wall from a low start.

1. 🟡 **(6b+) Australia Roof**
   Traverse the break L-R under the roof, exit through the middle of the roof.

2. 🟡 **(6b)**
   The middle of the roof from jugs at the back.

3. 🟡 **(6c+) Australia Arete**
   SDS. Climb the arete, traverse left on slopers to finish up problem 1. Finishing direct up the arete is 6b.

4. 🟡 **(6a+)**
   SDS. The wall right of the arete.

5. 🟡 **(6a+)**
   Just right of the roof is a nice technical wall problem up the middle of the buttress.

Dave Buchanan on Dave's Groove: Steve Dunning

Area 5: The Pinnacle

5.1 Pinnacle Wall

5.2 The Pinnacle

5.3 Underworld

5.4 Close Range

5.5 Hanging Arete

Area 5.1: Pinnacle Wall

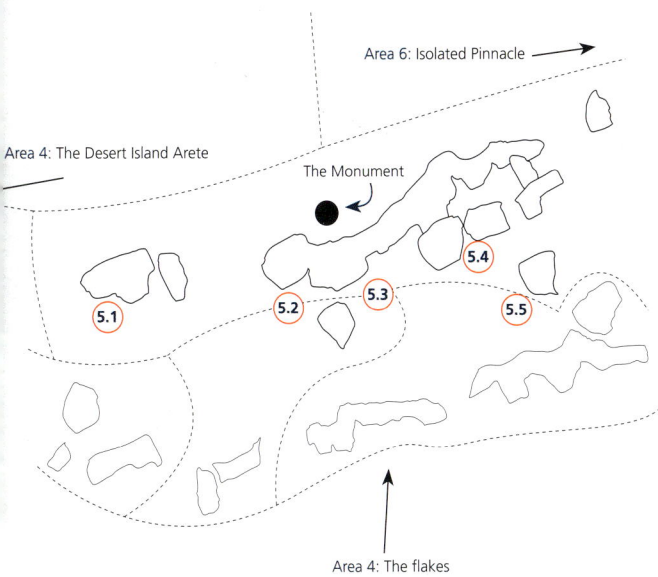

1. 🔵 **(4) Pinnacle Wall**
   The slab left of the wall.

2. 🔵 **(4+) Pinnacle Groove**
   The clean groove.

3. 🔴 **(7b) Back in Black**
   The centre of the wall. Climbed from crouching start at 7c.

4. 🟡 **(6b+) Highway to Hell**
   The right side of the wall is reachy and is done with a jump start. Pulling on is better and harder 7a.

Below this block is a hanging prow teetering close to a nasty drop. This is home to **Blind Pew** 6c+ which climbs the prow from a SDS. and uses the crease/seam on the left to gain the top.

165

Area 5.2: The Pinnacle

Area 5.3: Underworld

1. ● (5) **Pinnacle Slab**
   The middle of the slab passing a pocket.

2. ● (4+) **Pinnacle Rib**
   Climb the obvious rib on the right-hand side of the slab.

1. ● (6c-7b) **Ape Index**
   The wall with the block. Very reachy.

2. ● (7c+) **Underworld** ✱
   The block on the left is in. Doing it without the block is harder, but still 7c+.

3. ● (7b+) **Underpants**
   The dynamic undercut arete.

Area 5.4: Close Range

Area 5.5: Hanging Arete

1. ● (6a)
   SDS. The right side of the arete.

2. ● (6a+)
   SDS. The shallow groove.

3. ● (6b+) **Weight Gain**
   SDS. The wall via the hanging flake.

4. ● (7c+) **Feel The Burn**
   SDS. The blunt arete trending rightwards to finish up the thin wall.

5. ● (7c+) **Close Range**
   From the break gain a small crimp on the arete before moving out left to poor pockets and a jump for the top edge.

6. ● (6c+) **The Rover**
   Start as for Close Range finish rightwards passing a thin break.

1. ● (7b+) **Synchro**
   SDS. The left side of the arete.

2. ● (6b+) **Hanging Arete**
   Tackle the arete on the right-hand side.

3. ● (4+) **The Scoop**
   Tricky short problem through the sandy scoop.

Area 6: Isolated Pinnacle

6.1 Big Block
6.2 Isolated Pinnacle

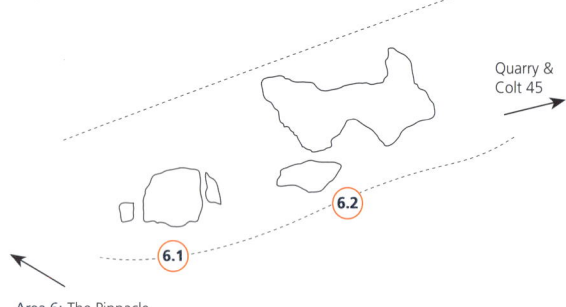

Area 6: The Pinnacle

Area 6.1: Big Block

1. ● (6a) **Phantom**
   The steep wall and left side of the arete.

2. ● (5) **Ghost**
   The easy angled wall.

3. ● (6a)
   The technical right side of the wall.

4. ● (6a)
   The technical right arete, climbed on the slabby side.

5. ● (6a)
   The flake right of the arete with a reachy rock-over at the top.

Area 6.2: Isolated Pinnacle

1. ● (6a) **Pinnacle Rib**
   The highball middle arete and rib.

2. ● (6c) **Pinnacle Edge**
   The right side of the arete is technical and quite bold.

Further right is a small quarry sporting a quality problem (7a+) tackling the technical wall just right of the left arete. It Involves a big gaston move for a good hold at the top of the arete. Picture Opposite.

Further right again the bouldering begins to disappear. However, the amazing **Colt 45** (7c) takes the stunning rounded arete just passed the quarry. Take the same arete on the left-hand side for a 6c tick.

Dvae Sutcliffe at Earl Crag: Steve Dunning

THE HITCHING STONE

Steve Dunning on No Mercy: Alex Messenger

The Hitching Stone

The Hitching Stone/Buckstone is a large single boulder near Earl Crag with a good selection of problems on excellent rock. The boulder has a number of quality problems in the mid to low font 6 range as well as a couple of harder testpieces. Classics such as The Runnel 6b and the superb prow, No Mercy 8a make the boulder well-worth a visit. The boulder is exposed and is best left for a calm, crisp day.

Approach and Access

Visible from the top car park of Earl Crag across the moor on the opposite side of the road. Approaching the crag involves dodging bogs and is best done in wellies or walking boots. From the gate walk direct to the boulder keeping close to the wall/fence. 15min.

THE HITCHING STONE

See the directions and parking for Earl Crag.

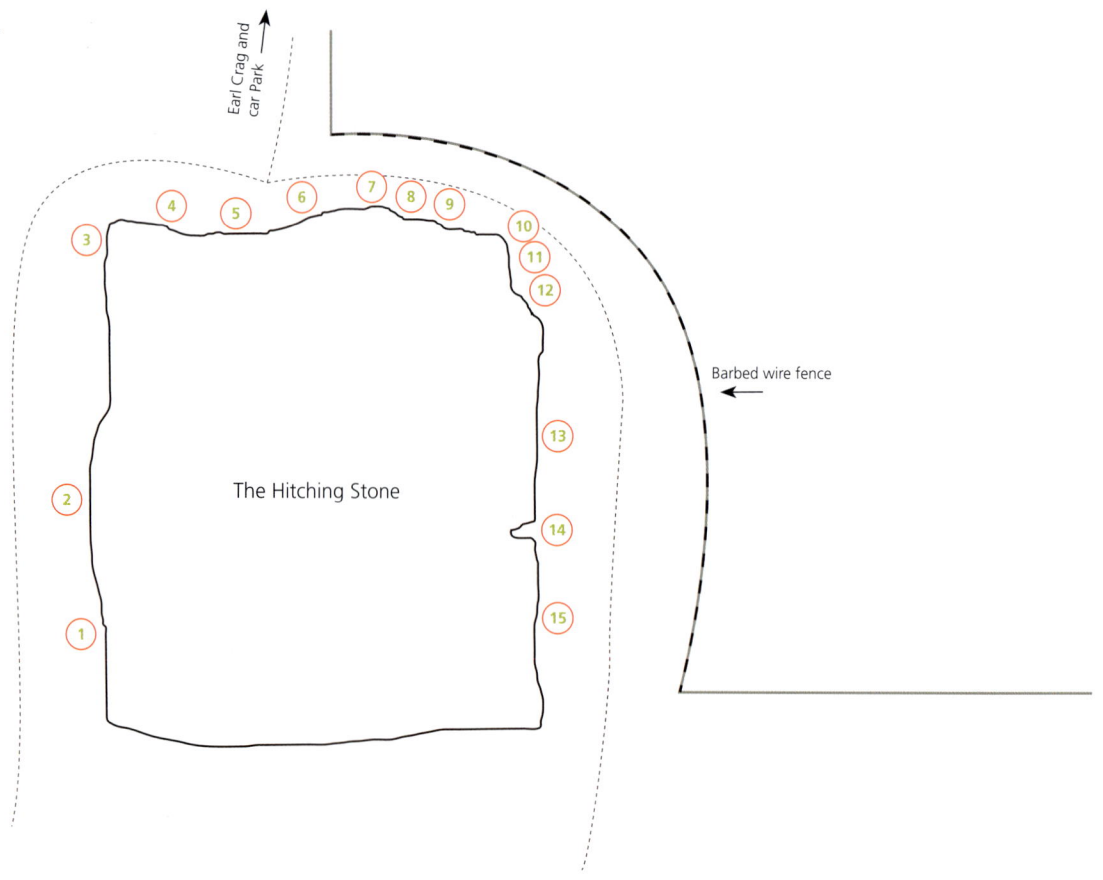

The Hitching Stone

1. ● (4) **Shattered**
The slab just right of the huge hole.

2. ● (4) **Hole Shot**
From the massive hole gain and climb the crack above.

3. ● (5) **Energizer**
The right side of the arete. The left side of the same arete is slightly harder 5+.

4. ● (6b) **Program**
The thin and technical scoop passing a positive undercut.

5. ● (5+)
Slabby groove.

6. ● (6C) **Missouri**
SDS. The blunt arete with a stiff pull off a flake.

7. ● (6a+) **Sole Trader**
SDS. The nice crack with good moves moving left to finish.

8. ● (6a)
Standing start from good hold on the lip, climb the bulging wall on good pinches.

9. ● (7c+) **Beatdown**
SDS. From the break make a big move up to a bad crimp on the lip before slapping up and right to join problem 8.

10. ● (8a) **No Mercy**
SDS. The steep prow. Start on undercut for right and poor crimp for left.

11. ● (6c+)
The steep prow from standing.

12. ● (7a+)
SDS. From the left gain the steep prow.

13. ● (7a)
Thin, eliminate wall between the crack and arete.

14. ● (5+) **The Crack**
Nasty.

15. ● (6b) **The Runnel**
Stretchy.

Bouldering, trekking, alpinism & other extreme outdoor activities

ALPKIT.COM

ILKLEY

Ben Bransby warming up at Ilkley: Adam Long

Ilkley

The local landmark of Ilkley crag dominates the affluent town below and also offers exceptional climbing. The problems on offer are diverse in terms of difficulty and style and are situated on the huge Cow, the smaller Calf, in the quarry and on several smaller buttresses. The northerly aspect of the crag and its position on the edge of Ilkley Moor can result in strong winds and low temperatures, it is fine in the summer but unbearable on a cold winters day. The rock dries relatively quickly and the steep front face of the Calf offers some degree of all weather bouldering.

Approach and Access

Visible above the town of Ilkley the crag is reached within minutes of the town centre. From the centre of town follow signs in the direction of Ilkley Moor. Follow the road (A65) up the hill until you reach the large car park on your right. 25 min. walk from Ilkley train station.

N.G.R. SE 130467

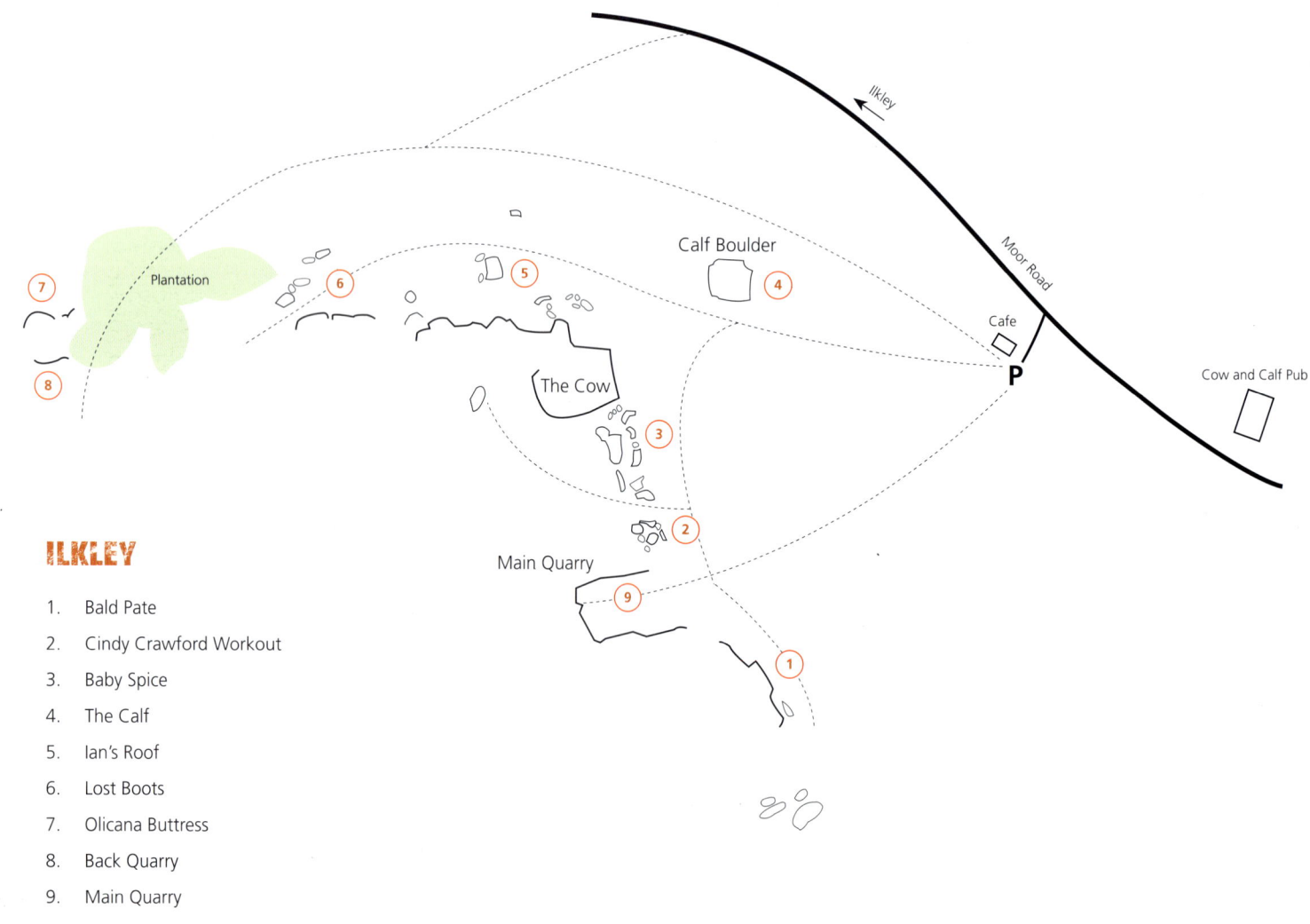

Area 1: Bald Pate

Area 2: Cindy Crawford Workout

1. ● (6b+)

   SDS. The arete just above the path.

2. ● (7b+)

   Start on the right and make a hard move to a vague crack. Finish up the slab.

3. ● (7b)

   The flake on the arete. Rock-over right onto the slab to finish.

1. ● (7b+)

   Dynamic problem using a chipped and a natural hold to throw for a pocket. Can be done with a low start coming in from the right making it hard for the grade.

2. ● (7b) **Bald Pate Superdirect**

   The right arete finishing up slopers and pockets up and left.

3. ● (7b) **Bald Pate Direct**

   SDS. Use a mono to gain the ledge.

Area 3: Baby Spice

 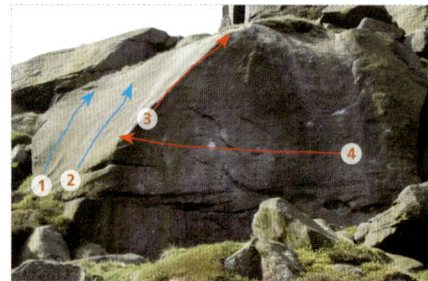 

1. ● (5+)
   SDS. Finish up the left side of the slab.

2. ● (6a)
   SDS. From the recess gain the slab and finish direct.

3. ● (6a+)
   SDS. Traverse L-R across the low break finishing up problem 4.

4. ● (6a)
   From the break climb the arete on the right side.

1. ● (4)
   The left side of the slab passing the graffiti.

2. ● (4-)
   The centre of the slab passing the graffiti.

3. ● (7b) **Baby Spice** *
   The arete climbed on its right-hand side.

4. ● (7a) **Ron's Traverse**
   R-L traverse from the chipped holds climb across the slab and around the arete. Keep feet on lower break.

1. ● (4+)
   The slabby left arete.

2. ● (6a)
   Direct up the slab. Avoiding the pocket and the slot is worth 7a.

3. ● (6b) **Flake Indirect**
   Use the flake to step onto the slab.

4. ● (6c+)
   SDS. Arete avoiding the slopey jug.

5. ● (6b+)
   SDS. The wall without the arete.

6. ● (6b+)
   SDS. The steep arete.

7. ● (6b)
   SDS. The right-hand prow/arete.

Above Area 3 is another quality boulder with a slopey traverse. From Area 3 walk up onto the moor, behind the Cow boulder. The problem traverses R-L on slopers and goes at 6c.

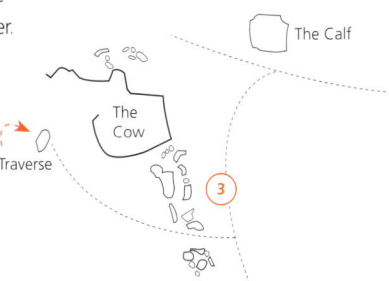

Lucinda Hughes on the back of The Calf: Dave Simmonite

Area 4: The Calf

1. 🟡 **(6b+) Facet Wall**
   The scooped wall and arete.

2. 🔴 **(7b+) Super Set** ✱
   Standing-start using the square-cut hole and small sidepull. Traversing in from low on the right is 7c+.

3. 🔴 **(7a+)**
   Start in the square pocket and use edges to gain the slopey top-out. The crack is out of bounds.

1. 🔵 **(5+)**
   The juggy highball arete.

2. 🔴 **(7b) Three More Reps**
   The vague crack-line passing old peg pockets to the big flake. Jump off or rock-over if you want the full tick.

3. 🔴 **(7b+) Calf Traverse**
   From the jam in the crack traverse the face rightwards at mid-height.

4. 🔴 **(7c+) Piccachu Challenge**
   The low-level traverse.

5. 🔴 **(7b)**
   SDS. From the undercuts use the pocket for your left and slap up and right to big sidepull. Finish up and right on the flake.

6. 🔴 **(7b+) Bernie The Bolt**
   The centre of the wall finishing up and left on the big flake.

Area 4: The Calf

1. 🟢 (8a) **Pebble Dash**
   The massive slab is possibly the hardest slab in this guide and certainly one of the boldest.

   The undercut right arete is home to a modern classic.

   1. 🔴 (7b/+) **Ringpiece**
      SDS. From the crack use pinches and slopers to hit the 'ring hold.' Hold the swing and finish with an easy rock-over.

For all the info. on eliminates on The Calf boulder visit:
www.total-climbing.com

Kev Avery on Ringpiece: Steve Dunning

Area 5: Ian's Roof

1. 🔴 **(7c) Bouling Farre Arete**
   SDS. Excellent little arete is rather brutal. Linking from the big undercut on Ian's Roof is 7c+.

2. 🟡 **(6c)**
   SDS. From under the roof move out right to holds on the lip and finish up the wall.

3. 🔴 **(7b+) Ian's Roof**
   Awkward traverse from right to left along thin edges, finishing up problem 2.

4. 🔴 **(7a+) Dave's Traverse**
   From the start of Ian's Roof move out left along slopey lip to a tricky mantle.

1. 🔵 **(4+)**
   Smear up the short slab and up over the nose.

2. 🟡 **(6b+)**
   L-R traverse across the slab and finish up the arete.

3. 🔵 **(5+)**
   The centre of the slab.

4. 🟡 **(6a+)**
   R-L low-level traverse finishing around the arete.

Sam Whittaker on Lost Boots: Dave Simmonite

Area 6: Lost Boots

1. 🔵 **(5) Lost Boots**
   SDS. From the big hole gain the line of chips up the clean wall.

2. 🟡 **(6c+)**
   Start as for problem 1 traverse right on to slopers to reach the crack.

3. 🔵 **(5+) Patience**
   The large flakes leading to the ledge.

4. 🔴 **(7a) Little Hole**
   From the hole reach up and right into the groove and a slopey top.

5. 🔵 **(5) Big Hole**
   The big hole and chips up to the ledge.

6. 🟡 **(6c) Doing The Business**
   The groove via the holes.

1. 🔴 **(7a+) First Arete** ✶
   The desperate but classic arete is maybe easier for the short. The sitter is a little harder but still the same grade.

2. 🔴 **(7c+) Curious Yellow** ✶
   Quality problem from Ben Moon. From the flake rock-up to the undercut, use a poor edge to throw for good hold way up high. The SDS. is 8a.

3. 🟢 **(8a+) Curious Yellow Right-hand**
   Desperate right-hand start. Use poor pocket and dish to rock-into undercut. Finish as for problem 2.

Area 7: Olicana

From Curious Yellow another area can be reached with a number of steep, quality problems. Follow a track to the good path that runs up from the road. Cross this path and after 30m a roof becomes prominent on your left.

1. ● (7c) **Squeeky Pop**
   From the good holds in the break make a hard slap for the rounded top.

2. ● (7a) **Olicana Arete**
   SDS. The right arete is a superb problem.

1. ● (7b+) **Ming**
   From the back of the roof turn the lip right of the arete via some tiny edges.

2. ● (7b+) **Chariots Of Fire Eliminate**
   R-L traverse of the lip, avoiding the back wall.

3. ● (6c) **Chariots Of Fire**
   SDS. R-L traverse of the lip until the undercut crack can be followed to the arete. Finish up the crack.

4. ● (6c) **Dunroamin**
   SDS. Tricky problem that climbs over the lip via some very polished holds at the right-hand end of the roof.

Area 8: Back Quarry

The Back Quarry is situated just behind Lost Boots area. The problems face south and tend to dry quickly. The slab at the right-hand end has some nice problems but crumbly rock at the top! Problems such as Chuck Norris and Steven Segal are excellent.

1. 🟡 **(6b+) Ilkley Bar Kid**
   The technical scoop finishing left.

2. 🟡 **(6c+) Steven Segal**
   Hard move to a hold on the lip. Use the chipped jug on the left to finish direct.

3. 🟡 **(6a+) Right Face**
   Committing moves up the arete to gain the ramp.

4. 🔴 **(7b) Chuck Norris**
   Hard move passing the small undercut with bad footholds. Named because "it's harder than Steven Segal".

5. 🟡 **(6a) Arete Right**
   Thin climbing passing the undercut. Reachy.

6. 🟡 **(6a) Blue Cock Wall**
   Hard start getting established.

7. 🟡 **(6a) Chips Today**
   Thin moves passing the undercut.

8. 🔵 **(5+) Chips Arete**
   The right arete on the slabby side.

Other eliminates and some squeezed in problems exist in this area. You can download a topo at **www.yorkshiregrit.com**

Area 9: Main Quarry

1. ● (6b+) **Old Crack Arete**
   The polished arete right of the crack.

2. ● (6c+)
   Thin wall left of S Crack. From the chips make a dynamic move into the scoop.

3. ● (6a)
   L-R traverse across the slab using the breaks.

4. ● (6c+)
   Low-level L-R traverse on polished slopey holds. Finish on the block in the recess.

5. ● (6a+)
   Tricky mantle onto the sloping ledge. Escape.

1. ● (7a+)
   Low-level L-R traverse. Move around the arete and finish up problem 4.

2. ● (6c)
   Thin blunt arete climbed on the right side passing a pocket.

3. ● (6a) **Short Circuit**
   Thin wall right of the arete.

4. ● (6c)
   Technical wall left of the crack system. The cracks are avoided.

5. ● (6a+)
   The wall right of the cracks. The direct is 6b.

6. ● (6a) **Spider Wall**
   Polished wall left of the arete.

7. ● (6a+) **Earwig Rib**
   The right arete. SDS. 7a+.

Ilkley Rocky Valley

Another area on the fringes of the main Ilkley Crag, offering a range of modern classics. The climbing is situated on the collection of boulders spilling out of the bottom of Rocky Valley Crag. This area is not particulary easy to navigate and can be rather frustrating on a first visit. However, a number of the harder problems are well-worth investing some time in, with the crag being home to a number of modern classics such as A Crimson Tear 8a, Frank 8a, The Italian Stallion 7b+ and the excellent Polar Haze 7b. The crag does have some worthwhile problems in the 6's but overall most of the quality climbing is hard. We have included the majority of the better quality problems although not every problem is documented. For those who are super keen to explore further, check out Yorkshiregrit.com for a full topo.

Approach and Access

Rocky Valley can be approached from two directions. From the main crag a good path runs from the top of The Cow to the obvious 'Rocky Valley' about 500m south west. Alternatively you can approach the crag directly from Ilkey centre. From the centre, a one way street 'Wells Road' leads directly to a path running up to White Wells. The crag is easily visible beyond the tea shop.

N.G.R. SE 122464

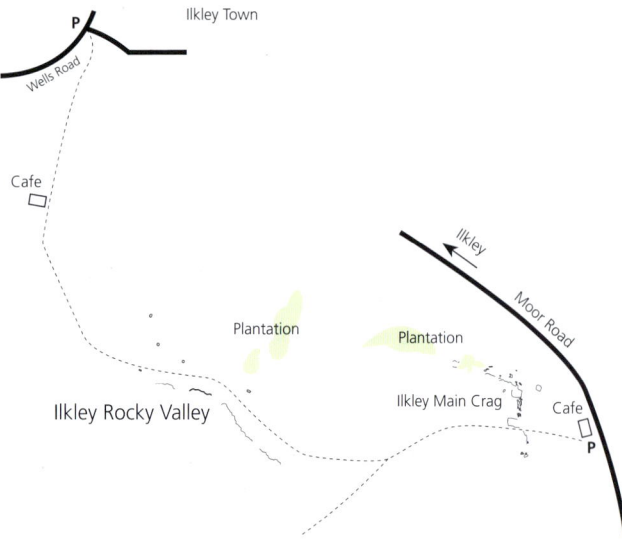

ILKLEY ROCKY VALLEY

1. Clubber Lang
2. Rocky Balboa
3. A Crimson Tear
4. Energy Follows Thought
5. Carnivore Roaming
6. Polar Haze

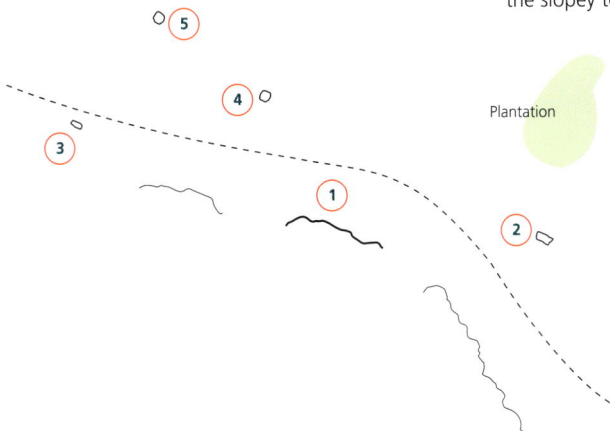

Area 1: Clubber Lang

1. ● **(7b) Clubber Lang** ✱
   Dyno from the large undercut to the slopey top.

Area 2: Rocky Balboa

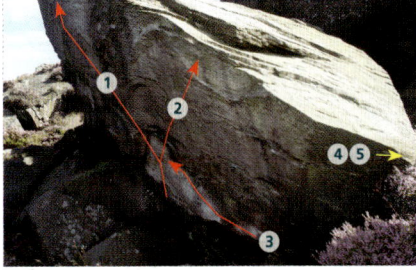

1. ● **(7a) Rocky**
   SDS. Starting in the pit with the block for feet. Crimp up the wall leftwards.

2. ● **(7b+) The Italian Stallion**
   Same start as Rocky but this time finish up and right.

3. ● **(7c) Rocky Balboa**
   Super low start in the pit hugging the prow and avoiding the block for feet. Crimp up and left to join problem 1 and finish up this.

4. ● **(6a) Jim's Problem**
   The arete on the right of the block.

5. ● **(6a+) The Big Wall**
   The middle of the undercut wall.

Area 3: A Crimson Tear

1. ● (7c+) **A Crimson Tear**
   Use a poor mono to make a dynamic move to the pocket and finish leftwards.

2. ● (8a) **Sweet Dreams**
   SDS. Hard moves up and right to a couple of positive edges. Slap up to vague pocket and finish direct.

Area 4: Energy Follows Thought

1. ● (7a) **Body Rocker**
   SDS. The scoop and arete passing a slopey hold.

2. ● (7b) **Energy Follows Thought**
   SDS. The scoop without the arete direct to the sloper.

Area 5: Carnivore Roaming

Area 6: Polar Haze

1. 🟡 **(6c+) Side Skirt**
   Climb onto the slab via the flake.

2. 🔴 **(7a+) Up The Skirt**
   Starting on two sidepulls make a hard dynamic move to the jug and top-out.

3. 🟡 **(6c+) Work Around The Skirt**
   Traverse the lip uphill.

4. 🔴 **(7b) A Carnivore Roaming**
   Traverse the lip rightwards finishing up the right side of the slab at the far end. Start on the chipped hold.

5. 🟡 **(7a) Carnivore Mantle**
   Desperate mantle onto the slab.

1. 🟡 **(6a) The Crimps**
   The short wall passing edges.

2. 🟢 **(8a) Frank**
   Use the slot to get established on the undercut wall. Finish with a hard move up and right.

3. 🟡 **(6c) Polar Direct**
   Climb the arete from the slot.

4. 🔴 **(7b) Polar Haze** ✱
   SDS. The tricky arete.

5. 🔵 **(5+) The Big Slab 2**
   The right-hand wall.

6. 🔵 **(5+) The Big Slab**
   The centre of the wall.

SWASTIKA STONES

Swastika Stones

Situated just above Ilkley on the north edge of the moor. Swastika Stones offers a small circuit of problems which are relatively quick to dry. The crag has a short approach time and makes for an excellent summer evening venue. Although the crag is not particularly extensive it does have a good selection of problems below 6c and a couple of harder problems up to 7b+.

Approach and Access

From Ilkley centre follow the main road towards Skipton. Turn left onto Victoria Avenue at the final set of traffic lights before leaving the town. Take a right turn at the T-junction (Grove Road) and follow this until it turns into a track and park at the far end of the plantation. The crag is just about visible through the trees. Take the track directly up the hill through the woodland until you reach the top wall. The crag is easily visible and a good path leads up to the first area described.

N.G.R. SE 095470

SWASTIKA STONES

1. Harris Slab
2. The Green Prow
3. Harris Arete
4. Barn Door Arete
5. Walking The Dog
6. The Badger
7. Jerry's Traverse
8. Tall Order Arete
9. Megalith

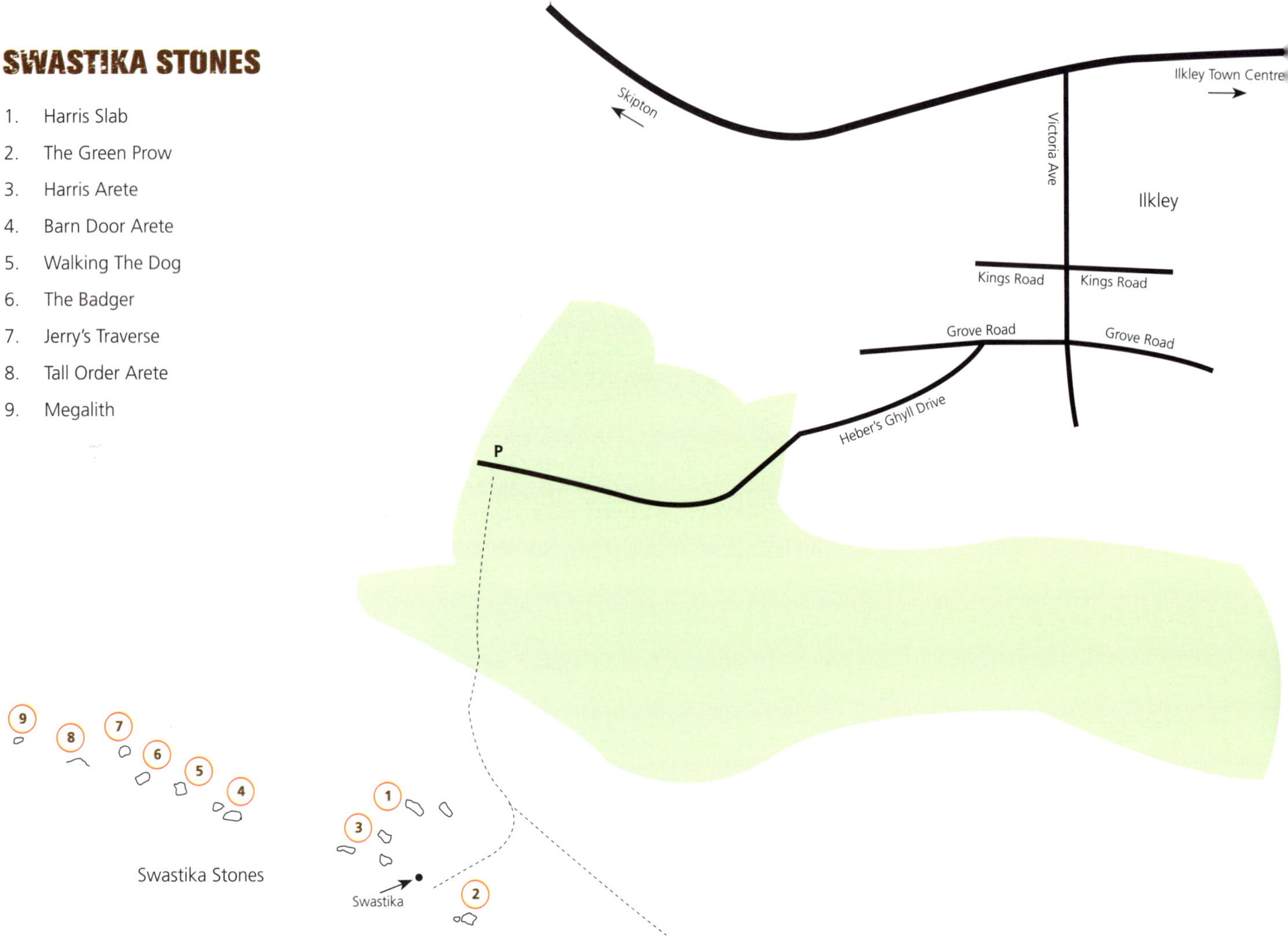

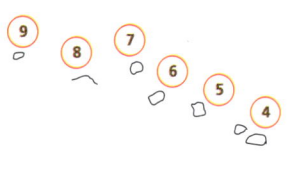

Area 1: Harris Slab

1. 🟡 (6a)
   Eliminate. The groove left of the slab avoiding a jug on the right wall but using a pinch above it.

2. 🟡 (6a) **Harris Slab**
   Thin climbing up the big slab.

3. 🔵 (5)
   Another good problem that requires a committed approach.

4. 🔵 (5+)
   SDS. The steep side of the arete.

5. 🟡 (6a)
   SDS. The wall right of the arete.

1. 🔵 (5+)
   The left side of the slab.

2. 🟡 (6a)
   The middle of the slab.

3. 🔵 (5)
   The left side of the sharp arete.

4. 🔵 (5+)
   Involving climbing up the right side of the arete.

5. 🟡 (6b+)
   Super thin moves on pebbles and poor crimps.

6. 🟡 (6a)
   The right edge of the slab passing a pocket and avoiding the arete.

SWASTIKA STONES

Pete Chadwick on Barn Door Arete: Steve Dunning

Area 2: The Green Prow

1. 🔵 (5+)
Highball arete usually green.

2. 🟡 (6a+)
Tricky moves up the short slab.

3. 🟡 (6b)
The steep prow on sharp but positive holds.

Area 3: Harris Arete

1. 🟡 **(6b) Slap Happy**
   SDS. Traverse L-R using the lip with unhelpful foot-holds.

2. 🟡 (6b)
   SDS. The overhanging arete.

3. 🔴 (7a+)
   Link problem 2 into a reverse of problem 1. Rocking onto the slab to finish.

1. 🟡 (6a) **Harris Arete**
   Smear up the short groove.

2. 🔵 (5+)
   The vague rib has some good moves.

SWASTIKA STONES

Area 4: Barn Door Arete

1. 🟡 **(6a) Christmas Day Arete**
   The left side of the arete.
   The right side is harder at **6a+**.

2. 🟡 **(6a)**
   The vague rib passing slopey holds.

1. 🟡 **(6a) Barn Door Arete**
   Exciting moves near the top.

2. 🔴 **(7b) Swastika Eyes**
   The super thin wall right of the arete. Dynamic.

Area 5: Walking The Dog

1. 🟡 (6c)
The centre of the wall. Very thin.

2. 🔴 (7b) **Pogo Arete**
The hanging right arete starting under the roof on dodgy flakes.

1. 🟡 (6c) **Walking The Dog**
Start on the shelf and traverse rightwards on good holds to a tricky move around and up the arete.

2. 🔴 (7b+) **Absconded Dog Extension**
Starting as for problem 1 continue around the arete, beasting up and along the poor slopers to a hard finish.

Area 6: The Badger

1. ● (6a) **The Badger**
SDS. The short arete using feet on the plinth at the back of the short roof. The mantle is the crux.

Area 7: Jerry's Traverse

1. ● (6c+) **Jerry's Traverse**
SDS. Traverse the lip R-L and finish rocking onto the slab.

Ryan Plews on Christmas Day Arete: Steve Dunning

Area 8: Tall Order Arete

Area 9: Megalith

1. 🟡 **(6a) Tall Order Arete**
   The right arete climbed on the left-hand side.

1. 🟡 **(6a) Slimeball Traverse**
   L-R traverse of the break below the top of the boulder.

2. 🟡 **(6a) Slimeball Arete**
   The arete.

1. 🟡 **(6b) Megalith**
   The right arete of the large slab above a poor landing.

Ilkley Pub Quarry

This compact quarry has a number of quality problems in a setting that is in stark contrast to the hussle and bussle of the main crag. Only a handful of problems exist here but for those who like technical climbing on clean-cut grit it's well-worth the stomp across the moor.

Approach and Access

The quarry is situated just over 500m from the Cow and Calf Pub behind and left of the main crag. The best approach is to follow the good track passing the left-hand side of Ilkley Crag. When you reach the top of the crag the quarry becomes visible in the distance. Alternatively park in the second lay-by after the main car park. From here the quarry is easily visible on the hillside above.

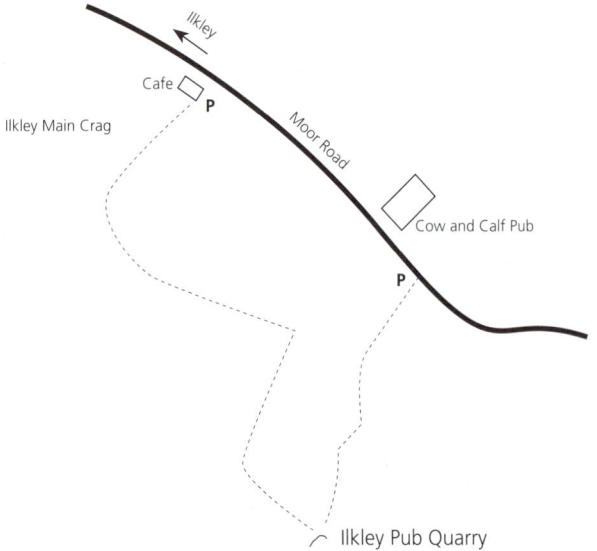

Area 1: Ilkley Pub Quarry

1. 🟡 **(6b+) Wreckedangle**
The clean-cut left arete. Start on the left, move right and then back left to finish.

2. 🔵 **(5+) The Ramp**
The ramp-line is a good test of balance.

3. 🟡 **(6a) Left, Right, Left**
The juggy flake-line just right of the ramp.

4. 🟡 **(6c) Happy Slapper**
The wall passing edges into the hanging groove and an exciting finish.

Nigel Poustie on Wreckdangle. James Ibbertson

SHIPLEY GLEN

John Dunne on Vim: Pete Chadwick

Shipley Glen

Situated on the moor above the industrial backdrop of Shipley the crag faces westwards and catches much of the afternoon sun. 'The Glen' offers quality bouldering with a distinctly urban feel. With the exception of Almscliff 'The Glen' has probably seen more bouldering traffic than any other venue in Yorkshire. This is mainly due to its proximity to Bradford and ease of access via public transport. For those that operate in the grade 5's the crag offers a wealth of technical classics, which tend to be big with good landings. However a couple of problems included are certainly worth a couple of 'E' points. Classics such as Manson's Wall 6c and Millstone Grit 7b are two of the best wall climbs around at their respective grades. Classic status also belongs to Mike Hammil's Red Baron climbed way back in '78 at 7a+ with the sit-start 7c+ added by Jason Myers some twenty years later.

Approach and Access

Situated minutes from Shipley and Baildon this is one of the few crags that is easily accessible by public transport. From Shipley follow Baildon Road and take the turning on the left to West Lane. Eventually picking up Lucy Hall Drive. This road ends at Glen Road. The crag is approached from either of the two parking areas on the map. From the North of Shipley (Ilkley etc) follow Sconce Lane and take the turning Bingley Road on the right just before entering Baildon. Glen Road is on the left after about a mile.

N.G.R. SE 131389

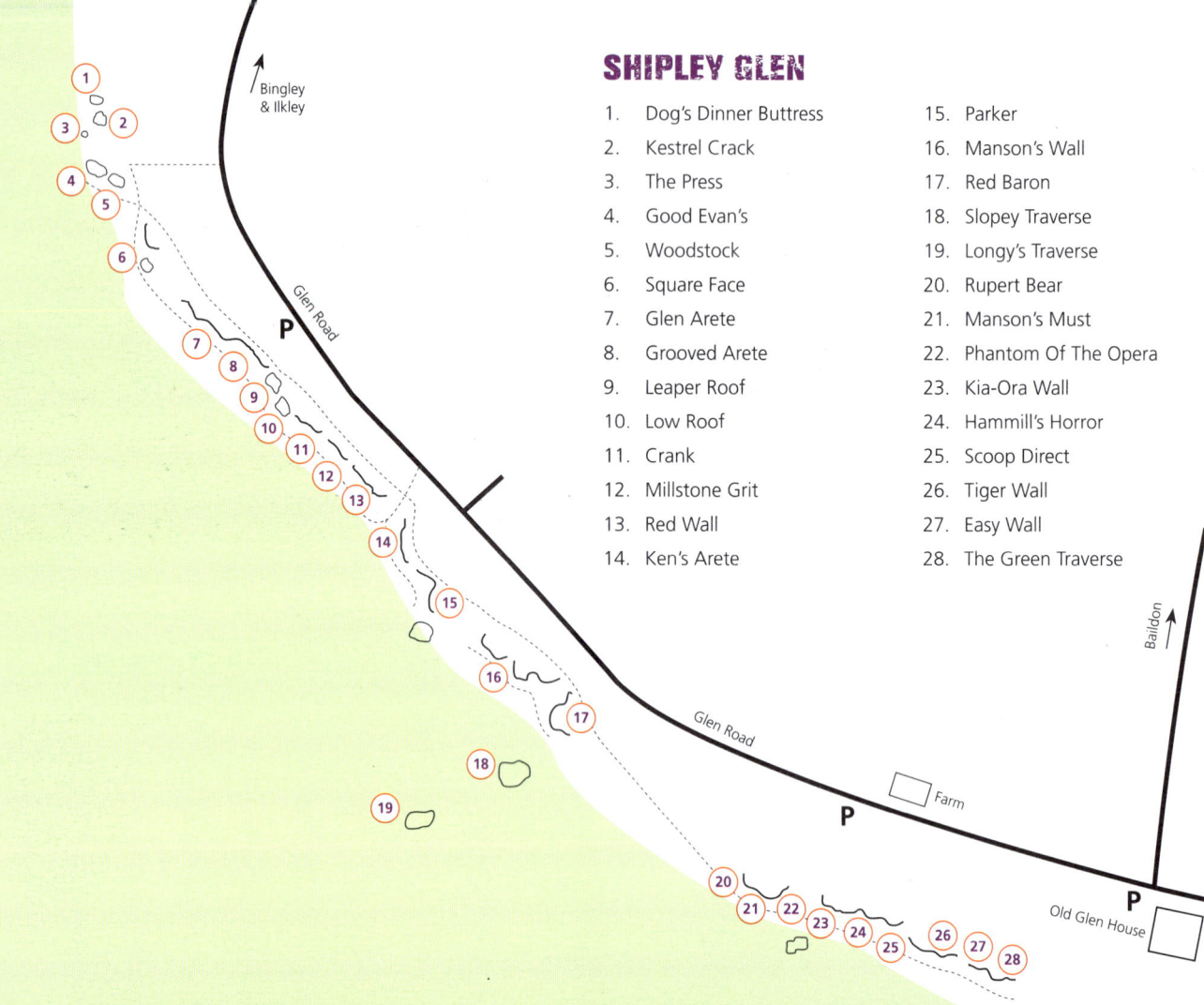

Area 1: Dog's Dinner Buttress

Area 2: Kestrel Crack

1. ● (5)
   The wall left of the L-shaped crack.

2. ● (5+)
   The wall passing the good break.

3. ● (4)
   The blunt arete right of the cleft.

4. ● (4) **Dog's Dinner**
   The wall between the blunt aretes.

1. ● (4) **Sparrow Hawk**
   The short wall left of the crack.

2. ● (5+) **Falcon**
   Fingery problem left of the hanging crack.

3. ● (4+) **Kestrel Crack** *
   The superb highball crack.

4. ● (5+) **Fowler**
   The imposing arete requires a confident approach.

Area 2: Kestrel Crack

Area 3: The Press

1. ● (5+) **The Blair Witch**
   SDS. From the cave pull onto the wall right of the arete. Climb the wall above direct, avoid the arete.

2. ● (6a) **Voodoo Doll**
   SDS. From the cave, follow slopers and good flakes rightwards. Finish up the right arete.

3. ● (4) **Christine's Horror**
   The wall above the graffiti passing a diagonal flake.

1. ● (4+) **The Press**
   From the arete rock-over onto the slab.

2. ● (6b+) **Low Block Traverse**
   The slopey lip traverse from R-L.

3. ● (3)
   The easy scooped wall.

Area 4: Good Evans

Area 5: Woodstock

1. ● (6a) **Double D**
   The steep wall climbed direct. Reachy finish.

2. ● (6c)
   The right side of the steep wall passing a perfect sloper. Finish up the right arete.

3. ● (6a) **Wall and Roof**
   The steep right arete with a tough move at the capping roof.

4. ● (4) **Hammer**
   The drifting crack.

5. ● (3+) **Leaper**
   The juggy undercut arete. Nice from a SDS. at 5.

6. ● (6a+) **Evans Above**
   Either make a big span from the break or use the side-pull to crank up for the break.

7. ● (6a) **Good Evans**
   The centre of the wall.

1. ● (4) **Rerun**
   The left-hand arete avoiding the vegetation.

2. ● (4+) **Linus**
   The flakey wall left of the crack. SDS. 5+.

3. ● (3+) **Woodstock**
   The prominent crack.

4. ● (5) **Lucy**
   The wall left of the arete avoiding the crack. Squeezed in.

5. ● (5) **Snoopy**
   Classic arete with a steep finish.

6. ● (5+) **Wooden Wedge**
   The wall right of the arete. Poor rock at the top.

7. ● (6a)
   SDS. Traverse R-L along the lip of the roof, across the crack and finish up problem 1.

Ewan McCallum on Donner: Pete Chadwick

Area 6: Square Face

1. ● (4)
   The undercut arete from the left. Escape from the ledge.

2. ● (5+) **One Hand One Hold**
   SDS. Over the roof and directly onto the ledge. Escape.

3. ● (4) **Central Route**
   The scooped wall passing a good undercut.

4. ● (4+) **Square Face**
   The wall passing slopey breaks.

5. ● (5+) **Layaway**
   The clean-cut right arete tackled on the left-hand side.

Area 7: Glen Arete

1. ● (4) **Last Line**
The wall just left of the arete passing a flake.

2. ● (5) **Revived 45**
The arete above the rock platform. Terrible landing.

3. ● (5+) **Fair Lady**
The wall right of the corner.

4. ● (6b) **Lancashire Hotpot**
The wall behind the tree. Bad landing.

5. ● (5+) **Mike's Wall**
The wall passing the flake. Nasty landing.

6. ● (6a+)
Squeezed in line between the flake and arete.

1. ● (4) **Glen Arete**
The big arete.

2. ● (4+) **YMC Wall**
The wall passing the flake.

3. ● (3+) **Groovy**
The centre of the wall.

4. ● (4+) **Faint Heart**
The juggy groove passing.

5. ● (4)
The small arete in the corner.

6. ● (4+) **Left Edge**
The wall passing the large rock scar.

7. ● (4) **The Hole**
The overlap above the hole.

8. ● (5+) **Chart Topper**
The curvy right arete.

9. ● (5+)
The crimpy wall inside the rift.

10. ● (4) **Golden Oldie**
The front of the block.

11. ● (4+)
The wall right of the arete.

Area 8: Grooved Arete

1. ● (4) **Golden Oldie**
   The front of the detached block.

2. ● (4+) **Stretch**
   Just left of the obvious groove.

3. ● (4) **Grooved Arete**
   The grooved arete.

4. ● (4+) **Reach For The Sky**
   Low start on the worn jug climb the wall passing slopey edges.

5. ● (5)
   The short wall from the sloper in the break.

6. ● (4) **Kate's Horror**
   The short arete left of the corner.

Opposite this area is a detached block with a superb traverse. Starting on the right edge before dropping onto the line of small edges. Traverse leftwards to finish on the clean-cut jug on the lip 6c.

This is a very short wall but the rock is good and it's a great spot for a quick warm up.

1. ● (4) **Stump**
   Short wall just left of the tree.

2. ● (4)
   The small wall right of the tree.

3. ● (3) **Gensing**
   The lay-back crack/corner.

4. ● (4) **John**
   The wall just above the 'John' graffiti.

5. ● (5) **The John Traverse**
   From the right arete traverse R-L below the top. Finish up problem 2.

6. ● (5+) **Wooden Wedge**
   The wall via the scoop.

Area 9: Leaper Roof

1. 🔵 **(5) Jug For a Thug**
   The left side of the roof.

2. 🔵 **(5+) Leaper**
   The big roof on good holds. Finish up the hanging arete.

3. 🟡 **(6a)**
   Starting up problem 2. Move rightwards under the roof and finish over the nose.

4. 🟡 **(6a) Lemur**
   Low start under roof, exit right.

5. 🟡 **(6a)**
   Traverse the break under the roof R-L to a tough finish up problem 3.

1. 🟡 **(6a) Leaper Traverse**
   R-L traverse using all holds below the top. Using holds below the overlap from halfway is 6b.

2. 🟡 **(6c) Leaper Eliminate Traverse**
   R-L traverse slopers before dropping down and using only holds below the overlap and avoiding the slot.

Area 10: Low Roof

Area 11: Crank

1. ● (6a+)
   The hanging arete without the back wall.

2. ● (6b+)
   SDS. From back of the roof climb out directly, finishing leftwards.

3. ● (6b)
   SDS. From back of the roof climb out directly, finishing rightwards.

4. ● (6b)
   SDS. The hanging arete from the back of the roof.

5. ● (7b)
   Start as for problem 5 traverse the lower break to finish up problem 1. Finishing all the way around the left wall is 7a.

1. ● (5+)
   The wall right of the crack.

2. ● (5+) **Crank**
   The wall passing the flake.

3. ● (6a) **Crank It**
   The wall via the sloping break. Start on the clean-cut jug.

4. ● (5+)
   The wall right of the worn jug.

Moving right towards the next area a steep prow becomes prominent below the path.

● (6b) **Rat Run**
SDS. From the crack move out left and finish up the arete.

Area 12: Millstone Grit

1. 🔵 **(4) Bonnie's Wall**
The wall just left of centre starting on the good break.

2. 🟡 **(6a) Adolph**
Climb the arete direct. Harder if you stick to the left side of the arete. Nasty landing.

3. 🟡 **(6b+) B-Team Traverse**
L-R traverse with hands in the mid-height break.

4. 🟡 **(6a) Donner** ✶
The undercut arete passing the square-cut ledge.

5. 🟡 **(6b) Rudolph**
The leftside of the big wall with a hard move near the top.

6. 🔴 **(7b) Millstone Grit**
Thin highball wall left of (and avoiding) the arete.

7. 🟡 **(6b+) Right Side Of Rudolph**
The wall just left of the arete. Avoid the arete.

8. 🔵 **(5+) Blitzen**
The right arete climbed on the left-hand side. Stretchy at the top.

Moving along is another buttress with a number of worthwhile problems. The undercut arete is the pick of the bunch.

1. 🔵 **(4+)**
The reachy wall.

2. 🔵 **(4+) Nicely**
The undercut arete.

3. 🟡 **(6a) Don't Fall Off**
L-R traverse from the crack to finish up the next problem.

4. 🟡 **(6a) Last Edition**
The steep wall, moving right to finish.

SHIPLEY GLEN

Area 13: Red Wall

1. ● (6b) **Circuit Breaker**
   Traverse top crack to arete then back along the bottom one.

2. ● (5+) **Lurcher**
   The smooth wall passing a slot. Start just above a small block.

3. ● (6a) **Lurch**
   The reachy wall above the slot.

4. ● (5+) **Red Wall**
   Keeping left of arete.

5. ● (5) **Cracked Rib**
   The right arete.

6. ● (4) **Flake Wall**
   The wall between the arete and corner.

7. ● (6a) **Hairline**
   SDS. The steep wall passing good edges.

8. ● (6a) **Prow**
   SDS. The undercut prow without stepping onto the opposite wall.

1. ● (4+) **Un-Original Route**
   Undercut prow.

2. ● (4+) **Banana Flake**
   The undercut nose passing the impressive flake.

Area 14: Ken's Arete

Area 15: Parker

1. ● (6a)
The wall with a tricky mantle into the flake, just below the top.

2. ● (5) **Funny Move**
Traverse break rightwards, finish up the arete.

3. ● (5+) **Ken's Arete**
The roof and arete at the left edge of the wall passing the sloper on the lip. SDS. 6a.

4. ● (6a+) **Mike's Mantle**
Reachy wall just left of the tree. Hard at the top.

5. ● (4+) **Green Wall**
The wall right of the tree passing the clean streak.

6. ● (5) **Green Arete**
The big right arete of the front wall.

1. ● (7b) **Honey I Shrunk The Kids**
SDS. From good hold under the roof climb out to the lip and cross onto sharp flake. Couple of stiff pulls to the good flake and finish more easily. The wall from standing is 6a+.

2. ● (7b+) **The Pinch**
SDS. Eliminate. Start under the roof and climb the blunt arete.

3. ● (4+) **Why Crack**
SDS. The strenuous crack. Moving out right is a tough 6a.

4. ● (7a) **Parker** ✱
The undercut arete, slapping leftwards to the slopey ledge. SDS. 7b+. Finishing rightwards up the arete is Lady Penelope 7b. SDS. 7c.

5. ● (5+) **Nosey**
Clamp up the nose.

Area 16: Manson's Wall

Area 17: Red Baron

Situated just below Parker.

1. ● (4)
   The left arete.

2. ● (4+)
   The centre of the slab.

3. ● (6b+) **Slab Traverse**
   R-L traverse keeping low under the ledge.

1. ● (6b) **OMO**
   The wall just left of the arete.

2. ● (6b) **DAZ**
   Technical arete with a committing move going for the top.

3. ● (4+) **Off Stump Wall**
   The wall between the corner and arete.

4. ● (6c) **Manson's Wall** ✳
   The wall passing tiny holds.

5. ● (7a) **Phil's Wall**
   The super thin wall, just left of the arete.

6. ● (6b) **Vim** ✳
   Ken Wood's technical masterpiece.

7. ● (6a) **Smear**
   The scooped wall.

1. ● (6b+) **Under Cracker**
   The wall between the two cracks.

2. ● (5+) **By-Pass**
   The right-hand crack line.

3. ● (6a+) **Amalgam**
   Connect problem 2 into the top of problem 4.

4. ● (7a) **Red Baron** ✳
   Another Mike Hammill classic from '78. Climbed on the left-hand side from standing. The arete on its right is 7b+ from standing and 7c+ traversing in from the ledge on the right. **Red Baron Roof** starts on the ledge at the back and goes at 7c+.

5. ● (5+) **Simian Traverse**
   The grinding ramp-line from standing.

Area 18: Slopey Traverse

Area 19: Longy's Traverse

1. ● (7b+) **Slopey Traverse**
   Climb down the opposite side of the boulder, around the nose to finish way up passing the tree. Few repeats.

Below Slopey Traverse is another excellent pumpy challenge. Easier but just as good.

1. ● (7a) **Longy's Traverse**
   Starting on the lower arete, traverse L-R to a hard mantle just after the vague corner.

John Dunne on Red Baron: Pete Chadwick

Area 20: Rupert Bear

1. ● (4) **Sam**
   The easy-angled arete.

2. ● (6c+) **Rupert Bear**
   Follow the crack up the black face.

3. ● (4) **Paddy**
   The right side of the wall passing good breaks.

1. ● (5+)
   Traverse L-R along the break to the far arete.

2. ● (5+)
   The left-hand side of the blunt arete.

3. ● (5)
   The blunt nose.

4. ● (4+)
   The wall with a big reach from the break.

Area 21: Manson's Must

Area 22: Phantom Of The Opera

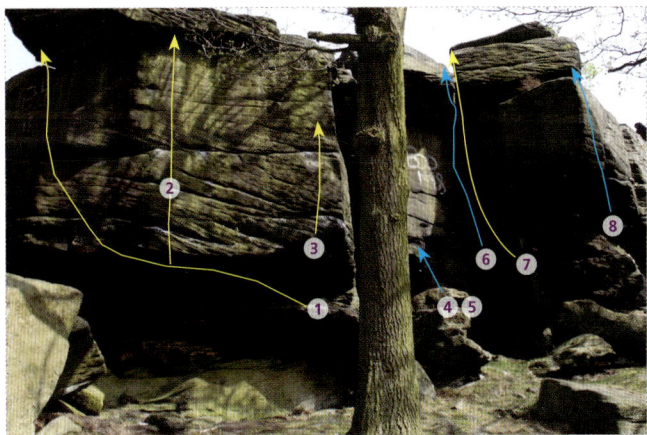

1. 🟡 **(6a) Al's Arete**
Small arete just right of the gully.

2. 🟡 **(6c) Vault**
The middle of the wall with a big wallop for the top.

3. 🟡 **(6b) Manson's Must**
Classic undercut arete with a terrible landing.

4. 🔵 **(5+) Raspberry**
The steep wall right of the corner.

5. 🔵 **(5+) Wood's Arete**
The leaning undercut arete.

6. 🟡 **(6a) Wood's Wall**
Undercut slabby wall with a slopey finish.

1. 🟡 **(6a+) Phantom Of The Opera**
SDS. Start on the low shelf on the right. Traverse leftwards through low roof to climb the blunt arete and roof above.

2. 🟡 **(6b) Phantom Wall**
The centre of the wall. SDS. 6a+.

3. 🟡 **(6a) Phantom Rib**
The short hanging arete. SDS. 6a.

4. 🔵 **(4) Phantom**
The wall right of the arete.

5. 🔵 **(5+)**
The small arete with a thrutch over the capping roof. Poor landing.

6. 🔵 **(3) Phantom Crack**
The often dirty crack in the corner.

7. 🟡 **(6a+)**
The left side of the crack/corner.

8. 🔵 **(5+) Saplink**
The steep prow passing the flake.

Area 23: Kia-Ora Wall

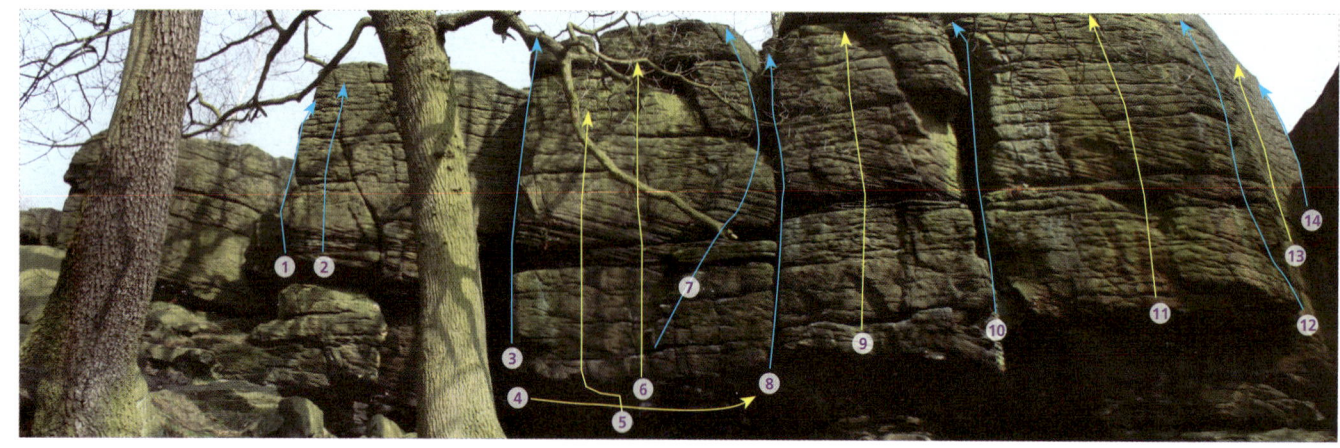

1. ● (4)
   Left-hand side of the arete.

2. ● (5+) **Green Death**
   The green wall left of the slanting crack.

3. ● (5+) **Next Arete**
   The undercut arete. SDS. 6a.

4. ● (6b+) **Green Traverse**
   L-R traverse keeping below the roof. Starting on the arete and finishing up problem 8.

5. ● (6b)
   SDS. The wall between the arete and the ramp-line.

6. ● (6a) **Step Down**
   SDS. Pull around the roof and onto the ramp. Finish direct.

7. ● (5+) **Step up**
   From the ramp gain the arete left of the crack.

8. ● (4+) **Old Crack**
   SDS. The grizzly crack.

9. ● (6a+) **Interstella Overdrive** ✶
   The wall between the two cracks.

10. ● (4) **Original Route**
    Another nasty crack.

11. ● (6c+) **Ethinococcus**
    Highball wall.

12. ● (5+) **Kia-Ora Wall**
    Gain the left arete from the crack-line.

13. ● (6b) **Brush Off**
    Start up the crack to a committing finish on rounded holds.

14. ● (5+) **Old Peter**
    The blunt highball rib at the back of the recess.

Area 24: Hammill's Horror

1. ● (6a) **Glen's Mantle**
   Mantle onto the shallow ledge and follow the flake/crack to finish.

2. ● (6b+) **Hammill's Horror**
   Highball classic that is certainly worth an E point or three. Sequency and reachy.

3. ● (5+) **Hand Me Down**
   Start up problem 4. Climb direct through the niche, up the wall to a rounded finish.

4. ● (5+) **Austin's Hangover**
   The blunt arete.

5. ● (6b) **Good Golly**
   Between the crack and arete.

6. ● (5+) **Jam Crack**

7. ● (6b) **The Nobbler**
   From the boulder climb the flake-line. SDS. 6b+.

1. ● (6a) **Nought to Fear**
   Avoid the ledge and chip.

2. ● (5+) **Fear Nought**
   The flakey groove-line left of the roof.

3. ● (6c) **Dreadnought**
   Pull over the roof and finish up the wall above.

4. ● (5+) **Pillar Rib**
   The big arete with a committing finish up the left-hand rib.

5. ● (5+) **Pillar Rock**
   The steady wall right of the arete. Getting a bit high for a boulder problem.

6. ● (4+) **Scoop Arete**
   Chipped, highball arete.

7. ● (5+) **Scoop Direct**
   The rib leading into the scoop. Without chipped holds 6b.

Area 25: Scoop Direct

Area 26: Tiger Wall

1. ● (5+) **Scoop Direct**
   The rib leading into the scoop. Without chipped holds 6b.

2. ● (4+) **Scoop**
   The leftwards trending scoop.

3. ● (3+) **Paddy's Saunter**
   The right-hand side of the slab.

4. ● (6a) **Flying arete**
   The arete without using the back wall for feet.

1. ● (5+) **Pirouette**
   The drifting flake up the steep wall.

2. ● (5+) **Wool Man**
   May require a dynamic approach from the shorter climber. Finish leftwards.

3. ● (6b+)
   The right arete of the prominent pillar.

1. ● (5) **Tiger Wall**
   Edges left of the graffiti.

2. ● (3+) **Shoddy Wall**
   Easy, lay-back flake and crack.

3. ● (6a) **Mouse Wall**
   SDS. Crimpy wall.

Area 27: Easy Wall

Area 28: The Green Traverse

1. 🔵 **(4) Easy Groove**
   The slabby groove and ramp-line.

2. 🔵 **(4+) Easy Wall**
   The wall right of the groove.

3. 🔵 **(4) Easy Route**
   The easy-angled wall between the two big cracks.

4. 🔵 **(4)**
   The blunt arete right of the large crack.

1. 🔴 **(7a) The Green Traverse**
   L-R traverse. Start at the left-hand end of the bottom wall, passing the tree to finish up and over the undercut nose.

Further along the edge of the valley is another boulder with a low roof. Black Roof has no quality problems but it does have a few hard ones. Unfortunately, the landings are as bad as the rock quality. However, for those who have skin to spare here are a couple:

1. 🟡 **(6b+)**
   SDS. The left side of the roof.

2. 🔴 **(7a)**
   SDS. Start under the roof on the left, move out rightwards to finish.

Slipstones

Slipstones is a magnificent crag situated high on the shoulder of the Colsterdale Valley. The crag consists of many small buttresses of the finest quality gritstone, varying in height from 3 to 9 metres. Bouldering mats have ensured that many of the micro-routes are now approached as boulder problems, however care needs to be taken as some landings are worse than they first appear. The climbing tends to be thin and technical with a good number of excellent arete problems and fierce wall climbs. Classic problems such as Lay-By Arete, Sulky Little boys and Micro Corner are as good as any problems on grit. The crag faces south, making it an ideal winter venue but in summer it can be too hot. Don't forget to sample a pint on your way home in the delightful brewery town of Masham.

Approach and Access

From the A1 take the turn off for Masham/Bedale. Drive through Masham passing a petrol station on your right at the top of a hill. Take a left turn sign posted Fearby and Healey. After the village of Healey take a small road on the right leading to the valley of Colsterdale. After a mile or so a hairpin bend is passed and a lay-by becomes clear on the right. There is room for seven or eight well-parked cars.

From the parking follow the track for 300m until you reach a gate. Once through the gate follow a good path directly up the hillside next to the wall. 50m below the crag a vague path cuts through the bracken leading to the first buttress of Sulky Little Boys. 15min.

N.G.R. SE 138821

SLIPSTONES

1. Sulky Little Boys
2. Lay-By Arete
3. Stainthorpe's Wall
4. Agra
5. Paul's Arete

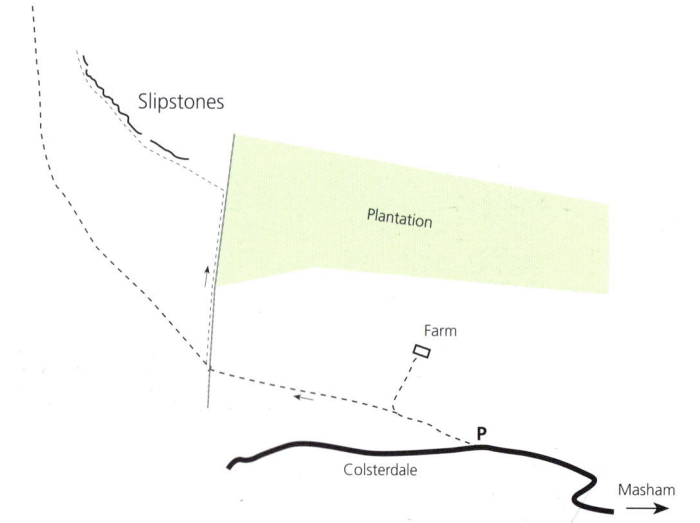

Note

Please do not drive up the track or block the gate. If the parking area is full a large parking area can be found 500m back along the road.

Area Guide

Area 1: Sulky Little Boys

SLIPSTONES

1. 🟡 **(6b+) Davies Ramp**
Quality arete with a tricky move high up. Start on the boulder.

2. 🔴 **(7a+) Simple Sally**
Direct Start to Davies Ramp. Avoiding the block and using small edges to gain good edges on arete.

3. 🔴 **(7b+) Holeshot**
Simple Sally to a thin rightwards traverse line. Finish up the right arete.

4. 🔴 **(7c+) Anniemutt**
From two poor edges in the middle of the wall throw for a good crimp on the traverse of Holeshot. Finish up the wall direct.

5. 🟢 **(8b) Cypher** ✱
Excellent hard arete. Reachy start.

6. 🟡 **(6b) Supple Wall**
Hang the sloper and make a tricky rock-over to the good flake.

7. 🔴 **(7a) Sulky Little Boys** ✱
Classic arete climbed on the right side. Avoid the pocket on the slabby wall for a 7a+ tick. SDS. Start on the right 7b+.

8. 🔵 **(4+) Slanting Flake**
Excellent flake line. Rocking out leftwards on thin holds into the small flake is 6c.

9. 🔴 **(7c+) Everything Counts**
SDS. The blunt arete (avoiding big flake) moving right on slopers to finish.

229

Area 1: Sulky Little Boys

1. ● (4+) **Welcome Wall**
   The obvious west facing wall on the far left of the slab.

2. ● (4+) **Stereo Android**
   The arete between the wall and slab.

3. ● (4) **Tommy's Dilemma**
   The centre of the narrow slab.

4. ● (4+) **Tea Party Slab**
   The centre of the slab starting right of the half height ledge.

5. ● (5) **A question Of Balance**
   From the left side of the lower ledge make thin moves up the slab.

6. ● (6a)
   From the middle of the lower ledge make a hard mantle using small crimps.

7. ● (5+) **Right Edge**
   The right-hand line on the slab starting on the right side of the lower ledge.

1. ● (6a+) **Bert Well's**
   The wall just right of the crack with a fierce first move.

2. ● (6a) **Centre Left**
   The wall just left of centre. Reachy.

3. ● (6a+) **Steptoe**
   The thin wall left of the arete.

4. ● (5+) **Tiptoe** ✱
   Excellent technical arete with barn-door move high up.

5. ● (6c)
   SDS. The wall opposite Micro Corner. starting on the low slot.

6. ● (7a) **Micro Machine**
   Tricky arete left of Micro Corner.

7. ● (6c) **Micro Corner** ✱
   The groove sorts the men from the boys.

8. ● (5+)
   The short wall right of Micro Corner.

1. 🟢 **(8b) Super Furry Animal**
   SDS. From edge and ear-shaped hold move up to sidepull and throw for the top.

2. 🔴 **(7b+) Sidewinder**
   SDS. From double undercuts move up and left to finish left of the capping roof.

3. 🟢 **(8a) Exocet**
   SDS. From double undercuts use opposing sidepulls to slap for sloper with left. Finish right of capping roof.

4. 🔴 **(7c) Stipule**
   SDS. From double undercuts move right to good lay-away, match this and throw direct to the top (no arete).

5. 🔴 **(7a+)**
   SDS. From double undercuts move right to good sidepull and throw for jug on arete.

6. 🟡 **(6a)**
   SDS. Superb sharp arete.

Steve Dunning on Super Furry Animal: Dalvinder Sodhi

Area 2: Lay-By Arete

1. 🔵 **(4+) Twenty Something**
   The wall left of the steep arete.

2. 🔵 **(5+) Overhanging Arete**
   The excellent steep arete.

3. 🟡 **(6b)**
   The centre of the wall with a dynamic move to a crimp.

4. 🔵 **(5) Flakey Wall**
   The line of creaky flakes.

5. 🟡 **(6c) Flakey Wall Traverse**
   R-L traverse of the crimpy break with poor smears, finish up problem 2.

1. 🔴 **(7b+) Lay-By Arete** *
   The excellent arete is a classic. Start on the right with a hard barn-door move to a good edge, finish swinging around arete at the good break. Direct finish staying on the right all the way is a committing 7c.

2. 🟡 **(6a) Lay-By**
   The classic curving flake line.

3. 🟡 **(6c) Little Baldy**
   The direct start to problem 4 is a stern test of finger strength.

4. 🟡 **(6b+) Rock On Left Hand**
   From the slot move up and left passing a pocket.

5. 🟡 **(6a) Rock On**
   The right side of the wall with a cool rock-over press move.

6. 🔵 **(5+) Rock Off**
   The right side of the arete.

Kevin Avery on Lay-by Arete: Steve Dunning

Area 3: Stainthorpe's Wall

Area 4: Agra

1. 🔵 **(4+) Fearby**
   The left-hand line.

2. 🔵 **(5) Stainthorpe's Wall**
   The centre of the wall, starting on the left.

3. 🔵 **(5+) Stainthorpe's Wall Right**
   The centre of the wall, starting on the right under the capping roofs.

4. 🟡 **(6a+) Fascinationby**
   The highball hanging groove.

1. 🟡 **(6a+) Friday The 13th**
   The blunt arete climbed on the left side.

2. 🟡 **(6b+) Sunday The Twentieth**
   The arete on the right side passing a poor pocket, starting direct.

3. 🟡 **(6c) Slipway**
   The blunt right arete is a superb problem.

4. 🟡 **(6a) Right Hand Twin**
   The wall and arete requiring good balance.

5. 🟡 **(6c+) Leaning Wall**
   The arete climbed on the steep side. The sitter is also excellent and is probably the same grade.

6. 🟡 **(6b+) Strictly Personal**
   The right arete passing a poor pocket. The SDS. is worthwhile and 6c.

Area 4: Agra

1. 🔵 (5+) **Cummin's Route**
   The wall just left of the crack.

2. 🔵 (5+) **Right Wall**
   The wall right of the crack.

1. 🔴 (7c+) **Twilight Session**
   SDS. The wall to the break via a big dyno.

2. 🟡 (6c) **Killer**
   Start up the groove and gain the break. Tricky moves above the break.

3. 🟡 (6a) **Ripper**
   The excellent high groove with a reachy finish.

1. 🔵 (5+) **Sowden**
   The slim groove is a classic.

2. 🟡 (6b) **Space Plucks**
   The highball wall moving right of the small capping roof to finish.

3. 🟡 (6b) **Sinbad**
   The highball classic passing a good flake.

Area 4: Agra

1. ● (6a+) **Impregnable**
   The high wall is best tricky near the top. SDS. Good thuggy start from under the roof is 6c.

2. ● (7b) **Self Suicide**
   SDS. The large flake in the roof is climbed from the back. Finish on the juggy break.

3. ● (4+) **Undercut Flake**
   The easy flake line is excellent, if a little high.

4. ● (5+) **Seven Up**
   The undercut buttress is a classic on perfect rock.

5. ● (5+) **Dennis In Darlo**
   The short vertical wall.

1. ● (5+)
   Climb the wall just left of the arete passing a pocket.

2. ● (6a+) **Timeless Divide**
   The twin aretes, with a committing move for the good break. Escape.

3. ● (6c)
   The right side of the arete, reachy move for the break. Escape.

4. ● (6c) **Agrete**
   The wall to the hanging flake. Escape.

5. ● (6a) **Agra Direct**
   The direct start to the classic route.

6. ● (5+) **Agra**
   Leftward rising line, finishing on good jugs.

7. ● (6c) **Wisecrack**
   The hanging crack climbed direct. Bad landing.

8. ● (7b)
   The wall right of the hanging crack passing the slot.

Area 5: Paul's Arete

1. 🟡 (6b+) **Original Traverse**
Excellent L-R traverse. Start at the far left end on the good break, keeping low finish around the right arete.

2. 🔵 (4+)
The crack to the good break.

3. 🔵 (5+)
SDS. The groove from a sitter is quality.

4. 🔵 (4+)
The shallow groove on nice slopey holds.

1. 🟡 (6a) **Paul's Arete** ★
The right side of the huge arete offers superb climbing on first rate rock.

2. 🟡 (6a) **Steve's Wall**
Another excellent, technical wall with some great moves way up high.

WEST VALE

West Vale

Situated on the edge of Greetland just outside Halifax, West Vale is a quarry which certainly has an urban feel to it. The crag is not particularly attractive but it has always remained popular with locals, due to its quality technical traverses and the endless eliminate possibilities. The majority of the climbing is crimpy on vertical faces with two steeper sections which are covered in holds and lend themselves to providing good eliminates. The crag dries quickly but can suffer seepage after heavy bouts of rain. The crag faces south.

Only the classics and more obvious lines have been included here.

Approach and Access

The crag is situated in Greetland which is just between Halifax and Huddersfield. From Halifax heading towards Elland on the A629 (Calderdale Way) take the exit for Stainland (Stainland Road). From the cross-road in the centre of Stainland take a right up Rochdale Road. After 300m turn right and park opposite The Star pub. Walk up the side of the pub (Wellgate) and follow Dean End dirt road until a gate is reached on the left. The crag is situated just beyond the gate.

WEST VALE

1. The Quarry

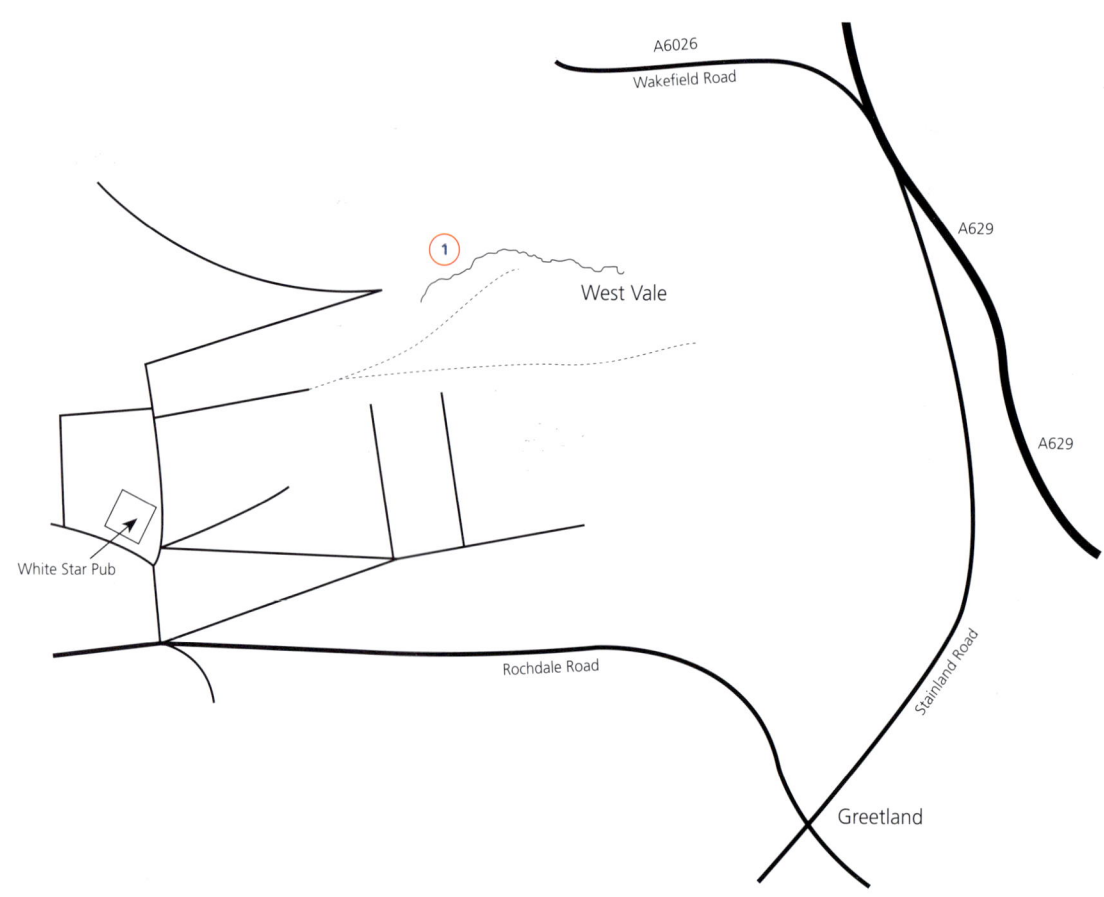

Area 1: The overhanging Face

Area 2: Rob's Arete

1. ● (6c)
   Low-level R-L traverse. Starting on Pig Farm Wall at the far end. Keep low all the way and finish up the arete.

2. ● (6c)
   Mid-level R-L traverse starting in the same place as problem 1. Keeping above the overlap.

3. ● (4+)
   SDS. The jagged arete to the ledge. Avoid the spike.

1. ● (6b)
   Low-level L-R traverse. Finish up the big crack.

2. ● (6b+) **Rob's Arete**
   The quality highball arete.

3. ● (6a)
   The wall right of the arete. Finish up the arete or move right onto ledge.

4. ● (6a+)
   The wall passing the sidepull. Finish on the left side of the ledge.

5. ● (6a+)
   The wall right of the sidepull passing small edges.

6. ● (6c+)
   SDS. From the bolt hole follow the arch leftwards before pulling over to ledge.

7. ● (6c+)
   R-L traverse. Keep low passing the crack, move up to ledge and finish around the corner.

Area 2: Butch's Wall

Area 2: Scott's Wall

1. 🟡 (6a)
   The wall between the two cracks. Avoid both cracks.

2. 🔵 (5+)
   The right-hand crack to the slot out right.

3. 🟡 (6b+)
   Low level L-R traverse. Start in the crack and finish at the chimney crack.

4. 🔵 (5+)
   The wall direct to the slot.

5. 🔵 (5+)
   The leftwards slanting rampline.

6. 🟡 (6b+)
   R-L traverse. From the chimney traverse leftwards at mid-height to the flake.

1. 🔵 (4+)
   The niche.

2. 🔵 (4+)
   The wall passing small edges.

3. 🟡 (6c)
   The centre of the wall.

4. 🟡 (6a)
   The wall left of the arete.

5. 🟡 (6a)
   The arete climbed on the left-hand side. Finish on the ledge.

6. 🔴 (7a)
   The right-side of the arete. Finish on the ledge.

7. 🔵 (5)
   Highball wall.

8. 🟡 (6a)
   The highball wall just left of the crack.

9. 🟡 (6a)
   Traverse the top break R-L. Keeping below the break is 6c.

Area 2: Scott's Wall

1. ● (6a)
The highball wall finishing up the crack.

2. ● (4+)
The good crack.

3. ● (4)
The wall passing the big flake.

4. ● (6c) **U2 Wall**
The wall between the flake and the arete.

5. ● (5+)
The quality arete.

6. ● (6a)
The wall just right of the arete.

7. ● (6c+)
The centre of the wall.

8. ● (6c+)
The wall left of the crack passsing the square-cut hole.

9. ● (6c+)
R-L low-level traverse.

1. ● (6a)
L-R traverse along the thin break.

2. ● (6c) **The Ramp**
The thin rampline trending rightwards. Committing.

3. ● (6a+) **Madness**
The wall above the 'M' graffiti.

4. ● (6c)
The wall just right of the GLYN graffiti.

5. ● (6a+)
Rock-over onto ledge.

6. ● (6a+)
Travesre R-L with hands at 3m all the way to join the second crack. Climb up to good ledge and continue around the arete. Traversing the whole crag **'Traverse Of The Gods'** goes from the same start and is worth 6c. Thats for the easiest route.

Whitehouses

Situated minutes from the road Whitehouses is a excellent little venue with a selection of high quality problems on first class grit. The problems are predominately roof climbs or steep aretes situated on two small south facing buttresses. Many of the problems share common starts and finishes and as a result the crag lends itself to providing excellent link- ups. Not the best venue for those not operating in the higher grades with many of the problems being at least 7a and the best problems are the hard ones. Due to its southerly aspect the crag is fast drying, for top conditions visit on a cold cloudy day.

Approach and Access

The crag lies just below the B6265 Pateley Bridge to Ripon road, about a mile outside Glasshouses. Limited parking (four cars) is available just opposite Cliffe Farm. From the parking, go through a gate then head across the field and down the hill for about 40m the crag is on the left.

Please ensure you don't climb over the gate.

N.G.R. SE 182651

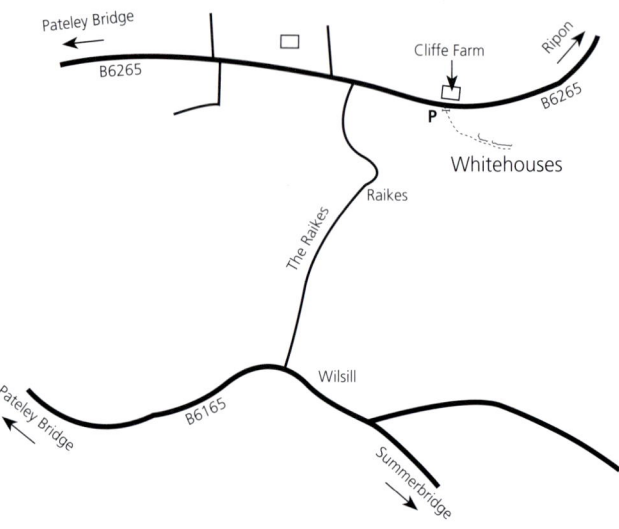

Area 1: Whitehouses

1. ● (7a+) **Rageh Omar**
The left arete starting on the lip.

2. ● (7b) **Under Rumsfeild**
SDS to problem 1. Start left of the arete avoiding the plinth at the back of the roof.

3. ● (6c) **Fat Punter'sRoof** ✷
The vague hanging arete from the lip.

4. ● (7a+) **Bush Bully**
The low start to problem 3. Starts on the two shot holes under the roof.

5. ● (7c+) **Whitefinger**
Excellent arete problem.

6. ● (5) **Central Crack**
The off-width chimney.

7. ● (7b) **Peg Leg**
Hanging start.

8. ● (7a+) **Peshmurga**
As for problem 6 but this time finish rightwards passsing a flake.

9. ● (8a) **Growled**
The traverse of the right-hand buttress. Start in central crack and traverse the lip (without any blocks underneath) to finish up Dubya. Starting at Peg Leg reduces the grade to 7c.

10. ● (5) **Dubya**
The right edge of the roof starting on the sloper.

Link-ups:

11. ● (7c) **Crazy Legs Crome**
Link of Rageh Omar into Fat Punter's Roof.

12. ● (7c+) **The Trial Of Slinky Bob's Master**
Crazy Legs Chrome into the jug on Fat Punter's Roof, then continue along the lip dropping down to the obvious holds at the right end of the roof. Finish up Central Crack.

13. ● (7c) **Kenny Boy Lay**
Follow Bush bully to the the big jug on Fat Punter's Roof and continue left to finish up Rageh Omaar.

Widdop

The tranquil setting of Widdop is home to perhaps the best circuit of problems in the area, classics such as Fight On The Black and The Seventh Wave being test pieces of the highest quality. The climbing is described as two distinct areas, the Main Edge and the Plantation Boulders. The Main Edge only offers limited quality bouldering, the best of which is included here. However, the Plantation area is superb with fantastic technical problems above nice flat landings.

Approach and Access

Plantation Boulders
The best approach for the Plantation area is to park at the large parking area at the east end of the reservoir. Cross the bridge to the dam and follow the good path around the reservoir until you arrive below the boulders on the edge of the Plantation.

N.G.R SD 934324

PLANTATION BOULDERS

1. First Boulder
2. Fight On The Black
3. Pickpocket's Wall
4. Four Square
5. Red Edge
6. Umpleby's Arete
7. The Big Crack
8. Seventh Wave

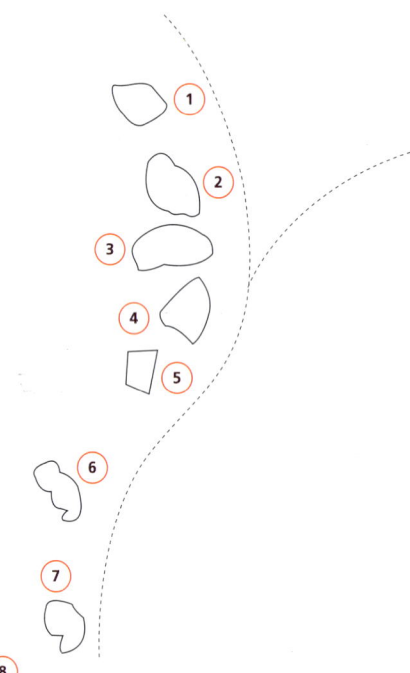
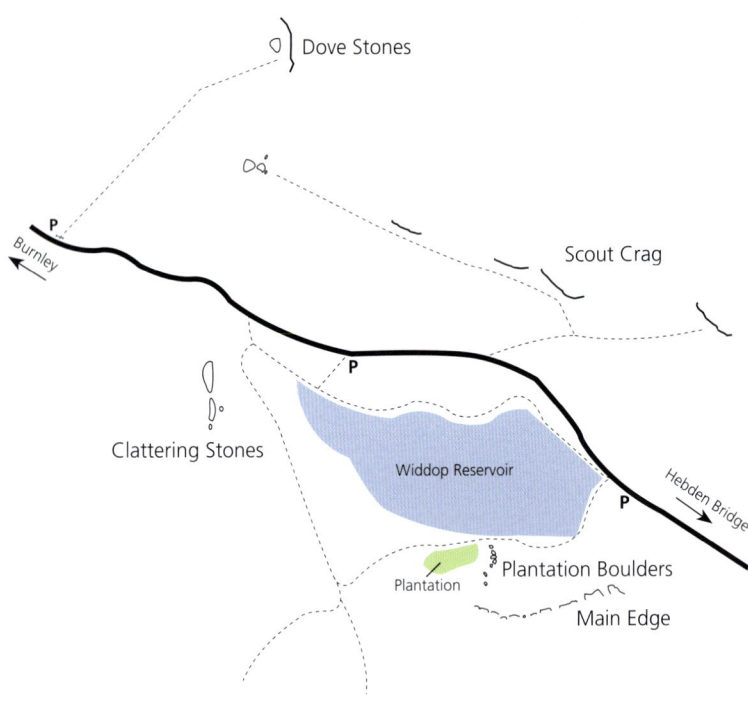

Area 1: First Boulder

1. ● (4+)
   The wide and awkward crack.

2. ● (5+)
   The hanging nose is a cool problem.

3. ● (6a)
   Nice climbing to the mantle with a slopey finish.

4. ● (5+)
   The arete.

5. ● (5)
   The centre of the wall.

Dave Parry on Fight On The Black: John Coefield

Area 2: Fight On The Black

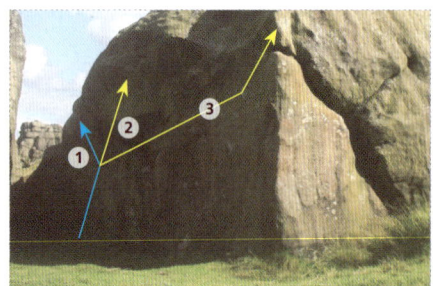

1. 🟡 (6b) **Splashdown**
   Superb, dynamic arete problem.

2. 🟡 (6c)
   The shallow groove in the centre of the wall via poor crimps. Reachy.

3. 🔴 (7b) **Fight On The Black** ✱
   The classic arete is one of the best problems at Widdop.

4. 🔴 (7b) **The Runnel**
   Tricky moves to gain the runnel right of the arete.

5. 🟡 (6b) **The Shelf**
   Start up the crack to gain poor slopers and a standing position on the shelf.

1. 🔴 (7a)
   The crimpy wall just left of the arete.

2. 🔴 (7?) **Three Pebbles And A Funeral**
   The line at the left side of the blank wall. Unrepeated since the demise of a hold.

3. 🟡 (6c)
   The line of slopers left of the shallow scoop.

4. 🟡 (6b)
   The reachy wall just right of the left arete.

5. 🔵 (4+)
   The left arete.

1. 🔵 (4)
   From the big hole exit via the crack and a slopey finish.

2. 🟡 (6a+)
   Undercut the hole and reach straight up. Reachy.

3. 🟡 (6b+) **Pool Traverse**
   Traverse right from the hole and finish straight up on slopers.

Area 3: Pickpocket's Wall

1. 🟡 **(6a) The Big Top**
   The left to right traverse of the top of the block.

2. 🟡 **(6a+) Pickpocket's Wall** ✸
   The superb central line just left of the crack and finish rightwards.

3. 🟡 **(6a+) Pickpocket's Crack**
   Stiff pulls on monos leads to the easy crack.

4. 🔵 **(5) Fagin's Ridge**
   The excellent right edge of the slab.

Right of the arete are a number of excellent highball slab problems.

1. 🔵 **(5)**
   The wall starting on the big sloper.

2. 🔴 **(7b+) Panic**
   The wall left of the arete passing some super thin edges to a big sloper.

3. 🟡 **(6b+) Four Square**
   SDS. The right arete climbed on its left-hand side. 6a climbed on the right.

4. 🔵 **(5+)**
   The centre of the wall passing tiny holds.

5. 🟡 **(6b+)**
   SDS. The wall left of the arete.

PLANTATION BOULDERS

251

Area 5: Red Edge

1. 🟡 (6a) **Red Edge Right**
   The arete climbed on the right-hand side.

2. 🟡 (6b+) **Red Edge Traverse**
   Start up problem 1 swing around the arete to finish up problem 3.

3. 🟡 (6a) **Red Edge Left**
   The left side of the arete.

Area 6: Umpleby's Arete

1. 🔵 (4+) **Umpleby's Arete** *
   The big arete is excellent but scarey.

2. 🔵 (4)
   The off-width.

3. 🟡 (6c+)
   Pebble pulling up the wall left of the crack.

Area 7: The Big Crack

Area 7: Seventh Wave

1. 🔵 (4+) **The Big Crack**
   The crack right of the arete.

2. 🔵 (5+) **The North Face**
   The slab right of the crack.

3. 🔴 (7a+)
   SDS. From the pod move left and finish up the arete.

4. 🟡 (6c+)
   SDS. From the pod slap up and right.

1. 🔵 (4)
   The right-hand side of the arete.

2. 🔵 (5) **Seven Deadly Sins**
   The left side of the slab.

3. 🔵 (4+) **Seventh Heaven**
   The centre of the wall.

4. 🟡 (6b+) **System 7**
   R-L traverse keeping low and finishing up problem 1. Harder if you drop down to the 'flattys' half-way across.

5. 🟡 (6a) **Seven Steps To Heaven**
   R-L mid-height traverse using the good foot-holds.

6. 🟡 (6c) **The Seventh Wave**
   R-L mid-height traverse using the slopey holds.

MAIN EDGE

1. Lip Traverse/Eliminate Boulder
2. Overhanging Buttress
3. Happy Feet
4. The Kidney Boulder

Area 1: Lip Traverse

Area 1: Eliminate Boulder

The main edge sitting above the reservoir is home to some excellent routes and a couple of classic problems. However, the crag receives little sun and can become very green. The bouldering is not particularly popular but we have included most of the quality problems.

1.  (6b+)
    Starting as low as possible traverse R-L along the lip and mantle at the apex.

Left and down from the main edge is an isolated boulder with a number of excellent technical problems. Not particuarly good for pure lines but lots of eliminates exist here.

Area 1: Overhanging Buttress

Area 1: Happy Feet

1. ● (6a)
   The slopey arete just left of the gulley.

2. ● (6b) **Brushed For Success**
   Climb the wall passing an undercut to a slopey finish.

3. ● (6b)
   SDS. From the scoop move up and right along the lip finishing right of the arete.

1. ● (7a+) **Pebble Love**
   The short wall is climbed via some tough pebble pulling.

2. ● (7c+) **Happy Feet**
   The super technical arete requires excellent foot-work.

3. ● (6a) **Dug Out**
   Low start on a pebble for the left hand and pinch for the right and go up passing a big sloper.

Area 1: The Kidney Boulder

1. ● (6c) **Zorro The Gay Blade**
   SDS. The wall between the two aretes starting on the left-hand side.

2. ● (6b) **Going Mantle**
   The prow via a tricep busting mantle. SDS. 7b.

3. ● (6b)
   Starting on the good ripple slap into the big pocket and top-out.

4. ● (6b+) **Corn Flake**
   From the flake climb the wall passing slopers.

5. ● (6c) **Red Rose**
   The right arete of the block from a standing start. SDS. 7b+.

Jordan Buys on Four Square: John Coefield

SCOUT CRAG

Photo: Steve Dunning

Scout Crag

The long broken edge opposite Widdop consists of three separate edges all of which are well-worth a visit. The problems are extremely varied with a combination of roof problems, slabs, rounded aretes and steep technical wall problems. This makes a day out at Widdop and Scout Crag a good combination.

Approach and Access

Scout Crag is also approached from the same parking area as Widdop. Walk along the road (eastwards) for approximately 100m until a good path becomes obvious at a small elevation of earth. This path contours up to the 'The Bay' area.

N.G.R. SD 933335

SCOUT CRAG

1. The Bay
2. Big Boulder
3. The Last Boy Scout
4. Boggy's Roof
5. Far Right

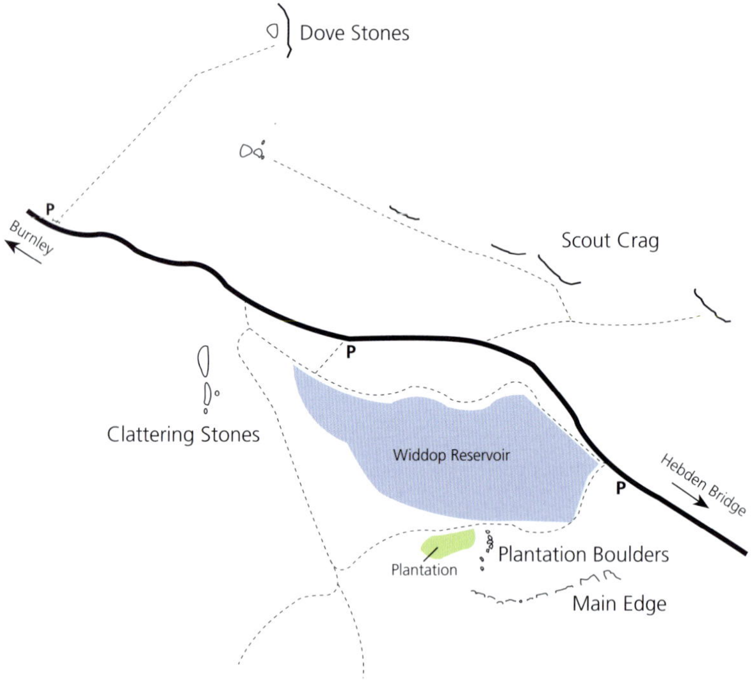

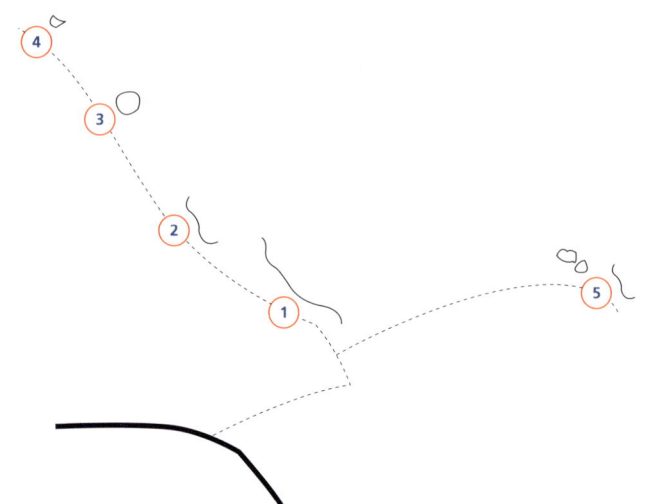

Area 1: The Bay

1. 🟡 (6a+)
   The wall right of the juggy arete. Harder than it looks.

2. 🔵 (5+)
   The juggy and awkward arete.

Moving around into the next bay.

1. 🔵 (5+)
   The slab via the rounded breaks.

2. 🔵 (5+)
   SDS. The low start to the crack just left of the slab.

1. 🟡 (6a) **Bay Arete**
   The steep arete with dynamic move to gain the large hanging flake on the right. SDS. Move up passing slopey boss via a couple of hard slaps 7a+.

2. 🟡 (6a)
   SDS. The nasty crack.

3. 🟡 (6b+) **Mantra**
   SDS. The thin wall from a sitter.

1. 🟡 (6b+) **Flaming Haggis**
   SDS. The arete and crack from the sandy sloper.

2. 🟡 (6c) **Flaming Lips**
   SDS. The wall just right of the arete via poor edges.

Simon Panton on Tall Order: Steve Dunning

Area 1: Bay Roof

Just behind Bay Arete is a nice low roof with a couple of excellent problems.

1. ● (6b) **Tall Order**
   SDS. From the back of the roof follow the line of slopey edges to the break and gracefully turn the lip.

2. ● (6b+) **Final Fantasy**
   SDS. From the break make a big move into the awkward crack.

   Other variations exist including linking problem 2 into the finish of problem 1 at 6c.

Area 2: Big Boulder

6. 🟡 **(6b+)**
SDS. From a poor edge make a powerful slap to a good incut, either match and throw for the top or move left and up. (easier)

7. 🟡 **(6a)**
Start hanging the incut edge and finish up and left.

Just down and left from the Big Boulder block is a delightful short slab with a nice 5+ left of the centre via a short hanging crack.

1. 🔴 **(7a)**
SDS. Big move from the slopey break into the flake crack.

2. 🟡 **(6a)**
SDS. The nose climbed direct.

3. 🔴 **(7a+) Big Boulder Wall**
Starting with right-hand on a lay-away and left on a lay-away or undercut slap up via slopey edges.

4. 🔴 **(7c+) Stone Rose Traverse ✱**
SDS. From the right arete traverse leftwards using edges in the break, finish up problem 5.

5. 🔴 **(7c+) Paranoid Android**
The crack is awesome. Pull on from standing, big move for a crimp up and right and throw for the top. Bad landing.

Area 3&4: Last Boy Scout/Boggy's Roof

The quality bouldering begins to peter out at this point. However, walk another 100m and you reach the excellent highball **'Last Boy Scout'** 6c+. The rest of the boulders in this area are worth a look but tend to be more route-like. If you still fancy some more you can continue to the far end and try the obvious **'Boggy's Roof'** 7b this takes the low roof direct from a low start. Starting in the same place but finishing rightwards passing the broken jug on the lip is 6c.

Dave Sutcliffe on Last Boy Scout: Steve Dunning

Area 5: Far Right

4. 🟡 **(6c) Midget Gem**
   SDS. Traverse leftwards across the lip and finish up the arete.

From The Bay area of Scout Crag a jumble of boulders can be spotted 150m to the right (looking in). Well-worth the stomp across the heather for a small circuit of quality problems.

1. 🟡 **(6b) Marble Man**
   SDS. From the back of the low roof reach around to a series of scooped pockets, traverse left and finish up the thuggy arete.

2. 🔵 **(5+)**
   The sandy wall with a tricky top-out.

3. 🟡 **(6b)**
   Excellent wall problem just right of the crack.

Futher rightwards are two excellent problems.

5. 🔴 **(7b) The Human Torch**
   SDS. Traverse right across the edges to a tricky finish on the arete.

DOVE STONES

Dave Buchanan on Pro Diablo: Steve Dunning

Dove Stones

Dove Stones is set in a lovely position overlooking Boulsworth Hill near Widdop reservoir. The crag is situated just above a breeding ground for Red Grouse in boggy acidic grasslands. This makes the approach rather tricky and it would be wise to approach in walking shoes. The crag consists of a broken edge along with a massive lone boulder. Excellent roof problems exist in close proximity to easy angled slabs with no shortage of technical aretes.

Approach and Access

Travelling west from Widdop reservoir a rusty barrier becomes visible on the right after approximately 1km. Park up without blocking the farmer's access to his land and take the obvious track through the gate for 15min. The track comes to an end at a circular site of an old ruin. From here the crag is clearly visible and a vague track runs up to the crag through the boggy grassland.

Note: Do not attempt to drive up the track as the farmer will lock you in! Also, consider that this is a valuable breeding ground, climbers must give due consideration. Dogs are not allowed.

N.G.R. SD 933348

DOVE STONES

1. Main Buttress
2. The Pinnacle
3. Low Roof

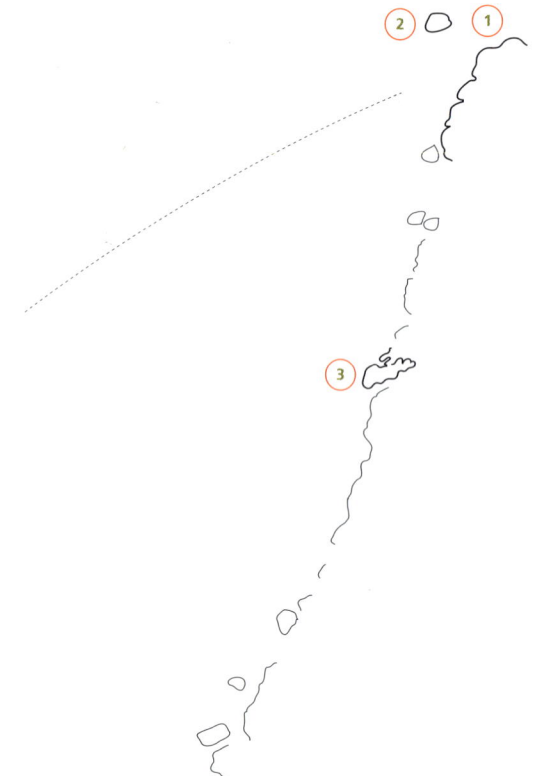

Area 1: Main Buttress

1. ● (6b+) **Clarence**
   SDS. Awkward but excellent arete. Start low on the right. Dynamic moves lead to the break.

2. ● (6b+) **Tempest**
   SDS. The bulge between the arete and the groove further right.

3.. ● (6b+) **Black Widow**
   SDS. Start below and right of the groove and climb the bulge up the groove's right arete

4. ● (7a) **Pro Diablo** *
   SDS. The nose of the buttress starting on the low break.

5. ● (7a) **Compound Bow**
   SDS. Start as for problem 3. Traverse right with feet up to finish up problem 4.

6. ● (6b)
   Traverse left on creaky flakes to a good edge and a worrying finale up the steep hanging arete.

7. ● (6a)
   Traverse the lip leftwards and follow the breaks above.

Area 2: The Pinnacle

Area 3: Low Roof

1. ● (6b+)
   The centre of the lower tier roof on jugs.

2. ● (5+) **Critical Care**
   The centre of the roof on the higher tier.

1. ● (6a+) **Mr Nobody**
   Just right of the overhanging face, climb the bulging wall passing a large sloping lay-away.

2. ● (6c) **Critical Care**
   The rounded wall right of Mr Nobody and left of a faint groove, from a sit start, to a scary finish.

1. ● (6c+) **Pinnacle Arete.** ✶
   Climb the left edge of the overhanging face to reach the handrail in the centre and a high finish.

2. ● (6c)
   Direct version of the arete, finish up the sloping breaks instead of moving right to the jug.

3. ● (6a)
   From the right end of the overhanging face, reach the handrail and traverse left into the centre. Finish on jugs.

1. ● (6c) **Boney Icarus**
   The crack on the right.

Dave Sutcliffe on Boggy's Roof: Steve Dunning

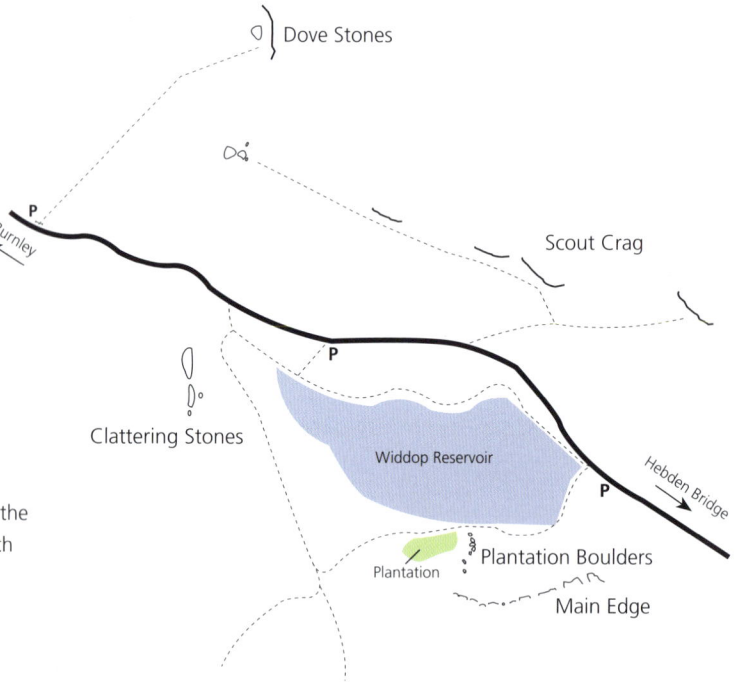

Clattering Stones

Although Clattering stones only offers limited bouldering potential the quality of the problems certainly make it worth a visit. Problems such as 'Love Handles' 6b+ and 'Morning Sickness' 6b are classics.

Approach And Access

Clattering Stones is reached by parking at a car park at the west end of the reservoir. Walk through the metal gate and follow a good track down the hill and across a small bridge. From here the two main boulders are visible on the left-hand side of the hill opposite. Follow a good track from the bridge for 50m in the direction of Widdop before cutting back and up via a vague track. The first boulder reached is 'Love Handles'.

N.G.R. SD 934324

CLATTERING STONES

1. Love Handles
2. Clatterjack

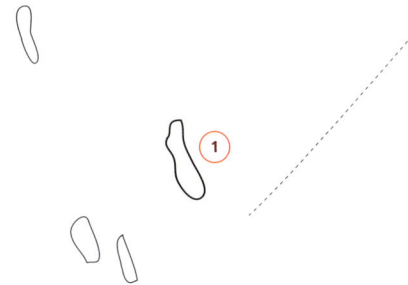

Area 1: Love Handles

1. 🔴 **(7a) Seconds Out**
   The prow provides an excellent test of squeeze-ability.

2. 🔴 **(7a) Poppy Arlington**
   The left arete of the boulder, stretching out right into the groove.

3. 🟡 **(6b+) Love Handles**
   The groove to the right.

4. 🔵 **(5) Early Learning Centre**
   The blunt arete.

Area 2: Clatterjack

1. 🔵 **(5) Clatterjack Toad**
   The sharp arete.

2. 🟡 **(6b+) Linea Nigra**
   The wall between the crack and arete.

3. 🟡 **(6a) Clatterjack Pencil**
   The thin crack.

4. 🟡 **(6c) Androsterone**
   The wall passed the flake.

5. 🟡 **(6c+) Fontanelles**
   The flakes further right.

6. 🔴 **(7b+) The Uprising**
   The arete is a classic.

GORPLE

Jon Pearson at Gorple. Chris Sims

Gorple

Gorple is situated behind Widdop Crag opposite Gorple Reservoir in an isolated position where solitude is guaranteed. Certainly a crag with many merits, quality rock, unusual formations and a spectacular view. The crag is situated a good half hour from the road and is very exposed to the elements so make sure you get a good forecast and take plenty of warm clothes etc. The crag is described here in two sections. Upper Gorple (Eternal Boulder) and Lower Gorple (Dicken Rocks). For those who are super keen Gorple Stones further up the valley offers a couple good problems but the main attraction is the hard unclimbed arete. This area is not included here as it is not particularly great.

Approach and Access

The best approach for Gorple is to take the good shooting track from a parking area 800m east of Widdop. The track takes a gentle route (700m) up to the edge of a reservoir. Take the path on the right passing a large plantation. After another 900m Lower Gorple becomes clear on the right just above a shooting hut. Upper Gorple is reached by continuing along the shooting track for another 300m before taking a track rightwards to the Upper Crag (500m).

Note: Please take note of any access restrictions during shooting season.

N.G.R. SD 931315

GORPLE

1. Eternal Boulder
2. Lower Gorple

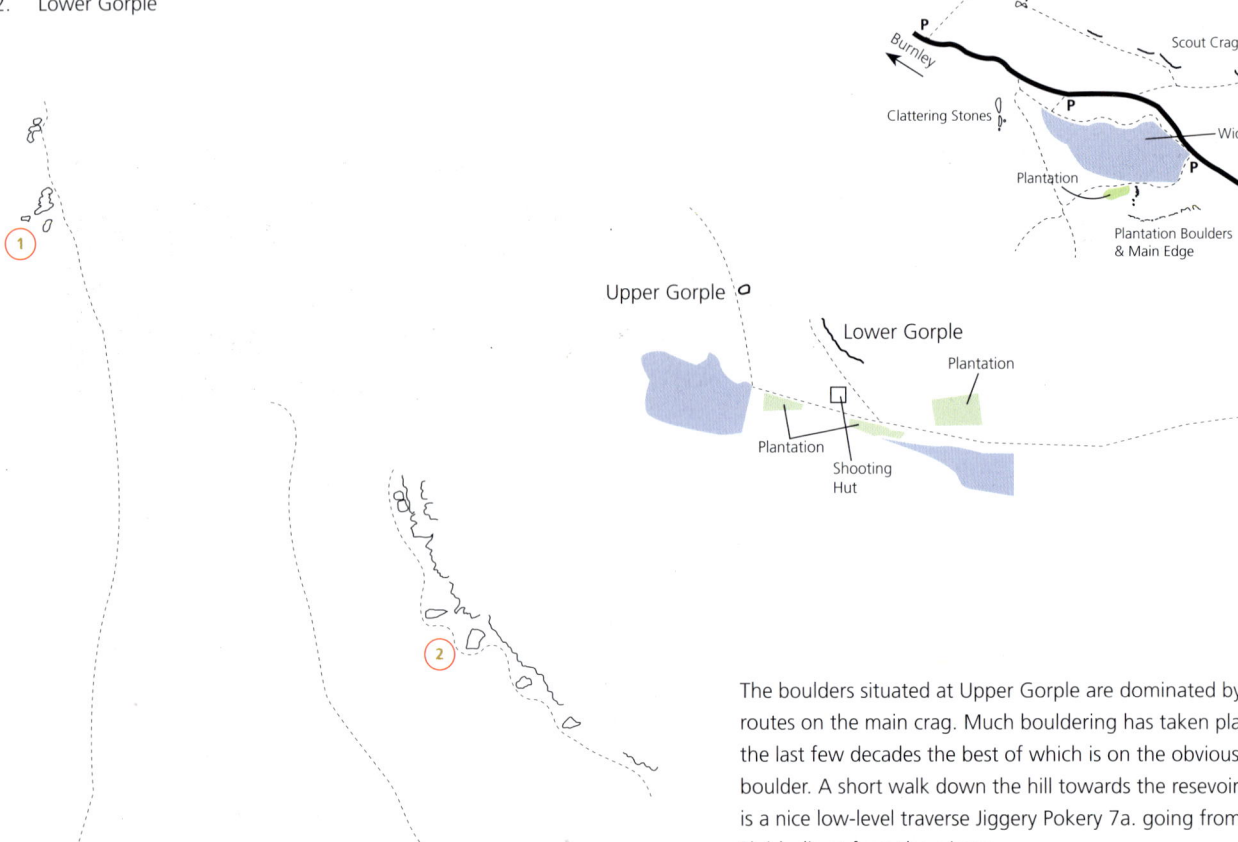

The boulders situated at Upper Gorple are dominated by the mighty routes on the main crag. Much bouldering has taken place here over the last few decades the best of which is on the obvious, large detached boulder. A short walk down the hill towards the resevoir is a nice low-level traverse Jiggery Pokery 7a. going from R-L. Finish direct from the crimps.

Area 1: Eternal Boulder

Area 2: Gorple Lower

1. ● (6b+)
SDS. Traverse the lip of the undercut slab on slopers to the arete. Rock-over onto the slab.

2. ● (6a)
The arete from a low start.

3. ● (6c)
The central line up the steep face.

4. ● (7a+)
SDS. Traverse the break from R-L. Finish just right of the arete.

5. ● (7a)
The direct line through the slopey break.

6. ● (6a+)
SDS. The crack.

7. ● (6a+)
SDS. The short wall just right of the crack.

1. ● (4+)
Smear up the short groove.

2. ● (3+)
Small arete.

3. ● (6a)
Narrow wall.

4. ● (6a+)
Wall next to the arete passing a slot.

5. ● (5+)
Gritty arete.

6. ● (6b+)
Gritty wall left of the fin.

7. ● (6b+) **Tender Hook**
The narrow fin. Tricky.

8. ● (6a) **The Tube** ✱
Delicate moves gain the bottomless tube.

9. ● (6c)
Technical wall via unhelpful pockets.

10. ● (3+)
Steady wall passing good but sandy holds.

Area 2: Gorple Lower

1. 🟡 (6b)
   Follow the scoops onto the arete.

2. 🔵 (3+)
   Steady wall passing a good break.

3. 🔵 (4)
   The wall passing the small capping roof.

1. 🟡 (6a) **Latest Trick**
   The hanging flake.

2. 🟡 (6b)
   Committing arete into the hanging groove.

3. 🔴 (7a)
   Gain the hanging groove direct passing the pocket.

4. 🔴 (7b) **Induction** ✱
   The highball arete with a bad landing. Can be sandy but excellent when clean.

Area 2: Gorple Lower

1. 🔵 (4) **Ripple Wall**
   Highball wall on good features.

2. 🔵 (4+)
   Nice moves up the easy angled wall.

3. 🟡 (6b+)
   The big slab with a couple of committing moves.

4. 🟡 (6a)
   The runnels and pinches up the right side of the big slab.

1. 🟡 (6a)
   SDS. The short flake.

2. 🟡 (6b)
   SDS. The wall on small holds requires a big span.

Area 2: Gorple Lower

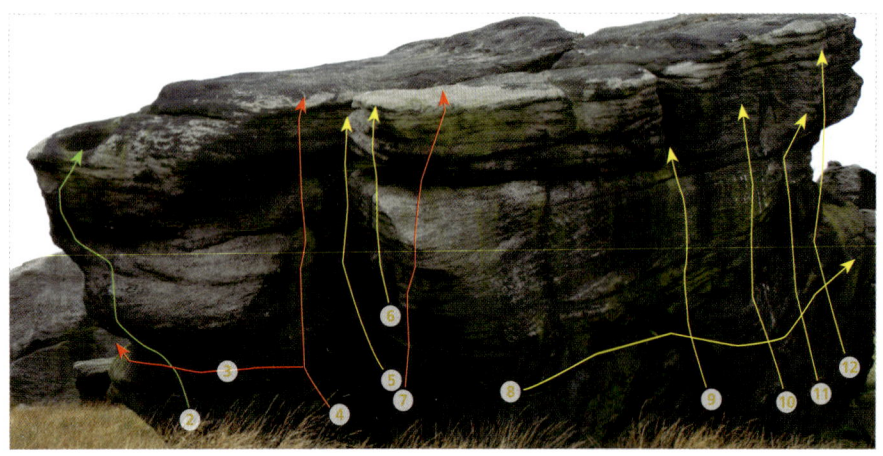

The awesome bulging prow is home to a couple of excellent hard problems. The slopey desperate Chebal 8a+ from Mark Katz is one of the best around. Take care on the problems 8-10 as the grades are a bit dubious and they are often out of condition.

1. ● (7a) **Escape from Postlovia**
The blunt left arete of the steep prow. Gritty.

2. ● (8a+) **Chebal** ✽
SDS. From the low edge on the right slap up and left to holds on the slopey shelf. Attack the bulge above passing some terrible slopers before reaching left into the crack/break and making a final couple of committing moves for the top.

3. ● (7c) **The Clangers**
The low R-L traverse from the crack around the steep wall to finish on the easy angled wall.

4. ● (7c+) **Cobra**
SDS. The bulging wall left of the crack passing a big boss and a vague crack.

5. ● (6a) **Ho Ho Ho**
The chimney crack.

6. ● (6c+) **I Am Not Spock**
The wall passing a broken edge to a slopey ledge. Escape left or finish direct.

7. ● (7a) **Trouble With Tribbles**
SDS. From the wall gain the rounded arete and a tricky finish.

8. ● (6b+)
L-R traverse to the far arete.

9. ● (6b+)
The vague corner. Tricky top-out.

10. ● (6c+) **Gareth's Wall**
Thin and reachy wall.

11. ● (6a+)
High wall into the scoop.

12. ● (6a+)
Highball wall with bad landing.

Area 2: Gorple Lower

Just right of the large sunken boulder is a broken buttress, split by a number of gritty cracks and breaks. The bouldering is not particulary inspiring on first appearance but it does offer good warm up potential with lots of problems between 3+ and 5+. Move along 30m and a number of better problems appear.

1. (?) **Flat Iron**
   Desperate mantle onto the hanging slab from a low start.

2. ● (4)
   Short juggy arete.

3. ● (6a)
   Start up the crack and finish over the small roof direct.

4. ● (4)
   Juggy breaks up the arete.

The next boulder is a little further along the track and is home to a number of classic problems. Most of the problems are from SDS. and require a long reach or a thick pad.

1. ● (6a)
   Left arete of the block.

2. ● (6c) **Sammy The Seal**
   SDS. Thuggy moves passing the rounded breaks.

3. ● (6c) **Ollie The Owl**
   SDS. The wall without using the arete.

4. ● (6c+) **Soul**
   SDS. Small but not insignificant arete.

Scout Hut 1 11 6 0

Situated between Widdop reservoir and Hebden Bridge. Scout Hut is a compact venue with some excellent problems. The crag benefits from having a number of problems that stay dry in poor weather, a popular 'plan b' venue for those caught out at the neighbouring Widdop crags. The crag faces south and is relatively fast drying. However, a number of problems are well-worth a visit in their own right. Classics such as Needle Of Dreams 7a and High Moon 6c being excellent problems. The climbing is varied but tends to be on the steep side, most of the classics being 7a or above.

Approach and Access

Travelling from Hebden Bridge, the crag becomes visible on the edge of a small valley 80m from the road at a series of hair-pin corners (500m before the Packhorse Inn). Limited parking (2-3 cars) is available opposite the Scout Hut Centre. Otherwise, continue up the road until parking becomes possible on the left after 100m. From the parking opposite the hut, follow the public footpath until a good track leads up to the crag.

N.G.R. SD 957124

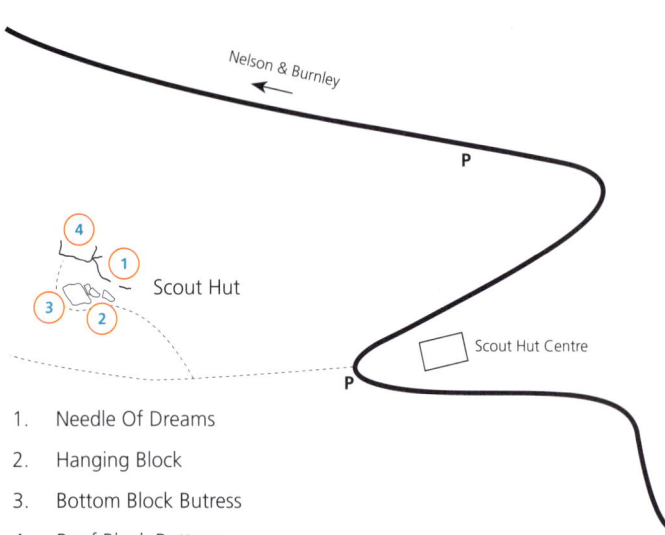

1. Needle Of Dreams
2. Hanging Block
3. Bottom Block Butress
4. Roof Block Buttress

Area 1: Needle Of Dreams

1. ● (6a+)
   The short slab approached from the left. The direct start is 6c.

2. ● (7c+) **True Torque** *
   The vague groove above the roof involves a hard move off a tiny edge and the diagonal sidepull to reach better holds and the ledge.

3. ● (7a) **Strone Road**
   Pull through the steepness to a pocket in the groove and make a committing move for the ledge.

4. ● (7a) **Needle Of Dreams** *
   The blunt nose above the roof climbed direct.

5. ● (6c) **High Moon**
   The right-hand arete passing the good flake.

Many good traverses and eliminates exist under the roof with the added advantage of being virtually weather-proof.

1. ● (6a)
   SDS. The undercut arete.

2. ● (5+)
   SDS. The crack up the centre of the undercut wall.

3. ● (6b+)
   SDS. The wall left of the arete. Avoiding the arete.

4. ● (6a)
   SDS. The right arete.

5. ● (6c+)
   R-L traverse. Start up problem 4 and traverse leftwards across the low break to finish up problem 1.

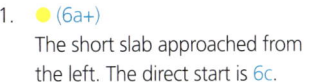

Area 2: **Hanging Block**

Area 3: **Bottom Block Buttress**

1. ● (6b)
SDS. From the low jugs under the roof, pull up to slopers on the lip and finish leftwards.

2. ● (7a+)
SDS. Reach up right to the slopey lip. Traverse rightwards and pull over the far arete.

1. ● (7a) **The Golden Fleece**
Starting low on a good hold around the right arete. Traverse R-L along the good low break, moving up to the middle then the top break. Continue to the far left arete and finish up this.

Area 3: Bottom Block Buttress

1. ● (7a) **Backfire**
   The steep arete on the edge of the cave. Low start using the arete and a crimp.

Area 4: Roof Block Buttress

Another boulder with a couple weather-proof traverses.

1. ● (6a)
   SDS. Juggy holds lead out rightwards and over the roof.

2. ● (6b)
   SDS. Traverse leftwards across break and finish up the sharp arete. Terrible landing.

3. ● (6b+)
   SDS. Traverse leftwards across break, continue along the middle break to the left arete.

4. ● (6b)
   Linking the low-level and mid-level traverses in either direction.

Mytholm Steeps

Mytholm Steeps is a little known venue on the opposite side of the valley from Heptonsall Quarry. The bouldering is not particularly extensive with only a handful of high quality problems scattered a short distance from the parking. The climbing can stay relatively dry in poor weather and along with nearby Scout Hut crag it offers a good wet weather alternative to Widdop and Scout Crag. Problems such as 'Not For Weasels' 7b+ and the traverse 'Wickerman' 6c are superb.

Approach and Access

From the centre of Hebden Bridge take the A646 in the direction Todmorden. Make use of the turning circle (direction Heptonstall) and turn left onto Church Lane. After joining Colden Road turn left onto the steep Bank Terrace which eventually turns into Glen View Road. The parking is just opposite a quarry after a hair-pin corner. From the parking (opposite the small quarry) walk down the hill to the hair-pin and cross the gate. Follow a good track for 30m until a vague track cuts across right to the first buttress. 5 min.

N.G.R. SD 980279

MYTHOLM STEEPS

1. First Boulder
2. Ghost Rider
3. Tony's Wall

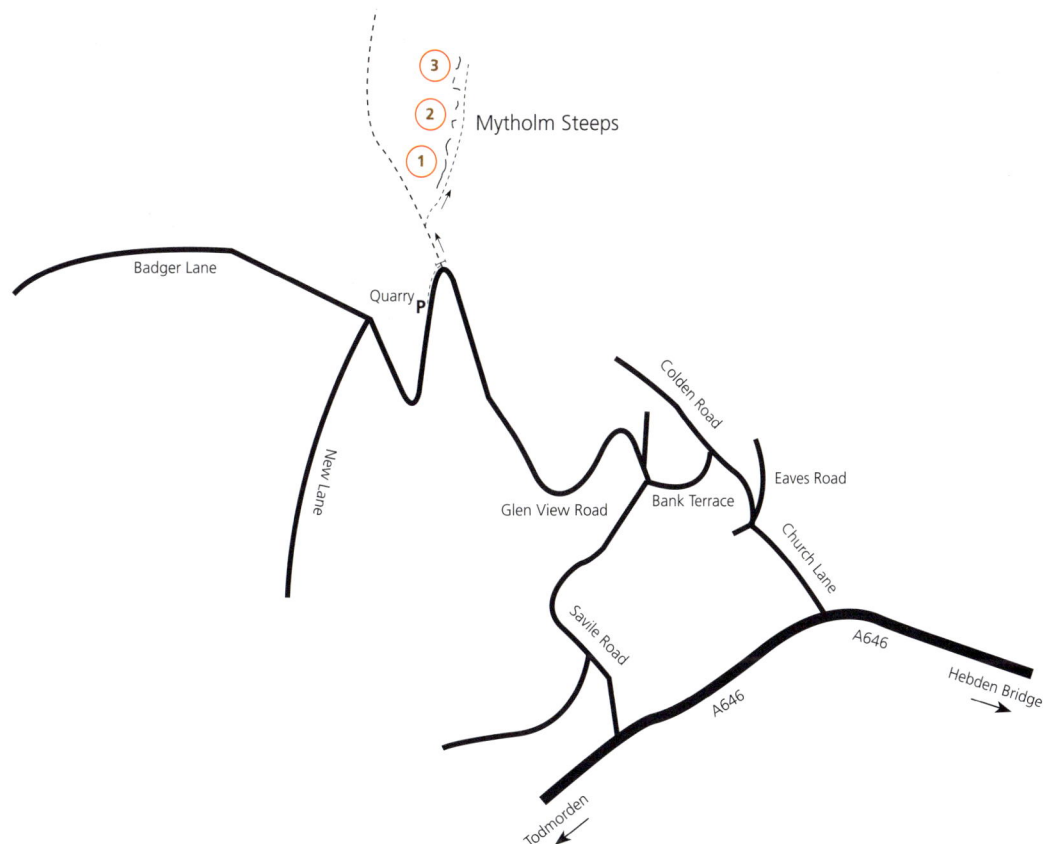

Area 1: First Boulder

1. ● (7b+) **Too Hard For Weasels** ✱
   The excellent undercut arete is destined to become a future classic. Thuggy climbing involving some nifty foot-work.

2. ● (6c) **Wickerman**
   From the right-hand end traverse left finishing up the often green arete.

1. ● (7c) **Gareth's Traverse**
   SDS. Traverse L-R pulling over the high arete. Start as low as possible.

2. ● (6b)
   The blunt arete requires a thrutchy approach.

Many other traverses and link-ups exist here.

Area 2: Ghost Rider

Area 3: Tony's Wall

1. ● **(7a) Ghost Rider**
   SDS. The rightwards trending curving rib. From the good holds at the start use a heel-hook to slap up the rib and finish rocking onto the slab.

1. ● **(7b+) Tony's Wall**
   The superb hanging wall on slopey pinchy edges. Trend rightwards after a stiff pull at the start. Sustained.

WOODHOUSE SCAR

Woodhouse Scar

Woodhouse Scar is a popular urban crag with easy access from Halifax and the surrounding area. Situated on the edge of the Calder Valley less than 2 miles from the centre of Halifax. Similar in style to Shipley Glen but not quite as extensive. The crag has a number of superb problems with a real mix of climbing styles. Roofs, technical aretes, and an abundance of highball wall problems ensures that every taste is catered for. The crag does suffer from a lack of respect from dog walkers as well as a problem with broken glass. Not the most child friendly of crags. However, classics such as Ian's Roof 7c, Piton Crack 6c, Poodle Wall 6a and Radium 6a+ would rate highly on any crag. The crag faces south.

Approch and Access

The crag is situated on the edge of Halifax and is best approached from the A646 (Skircoat Moor Road). Take the turning Albert Promenade and park in front of the bollards at the point where the road is blocked off. From here walk beyond the bollards and pick up the path on your right running down to the first area.

N.G.R. SE 083235

WOODHOUSE SCAR

1. Trackside Arete
2. Trackside Boulder
3. Spire Rock
4. Square Face
5. Upper Green wall
6. Poodle Wall
7. Pyramid Buttress
8. Slanting Clef
9. Piton Crack
10. Overhanging Group
11. Pebble Buttress
12. Cave Buttress
13. Slab Buttress
14. The Sheriff

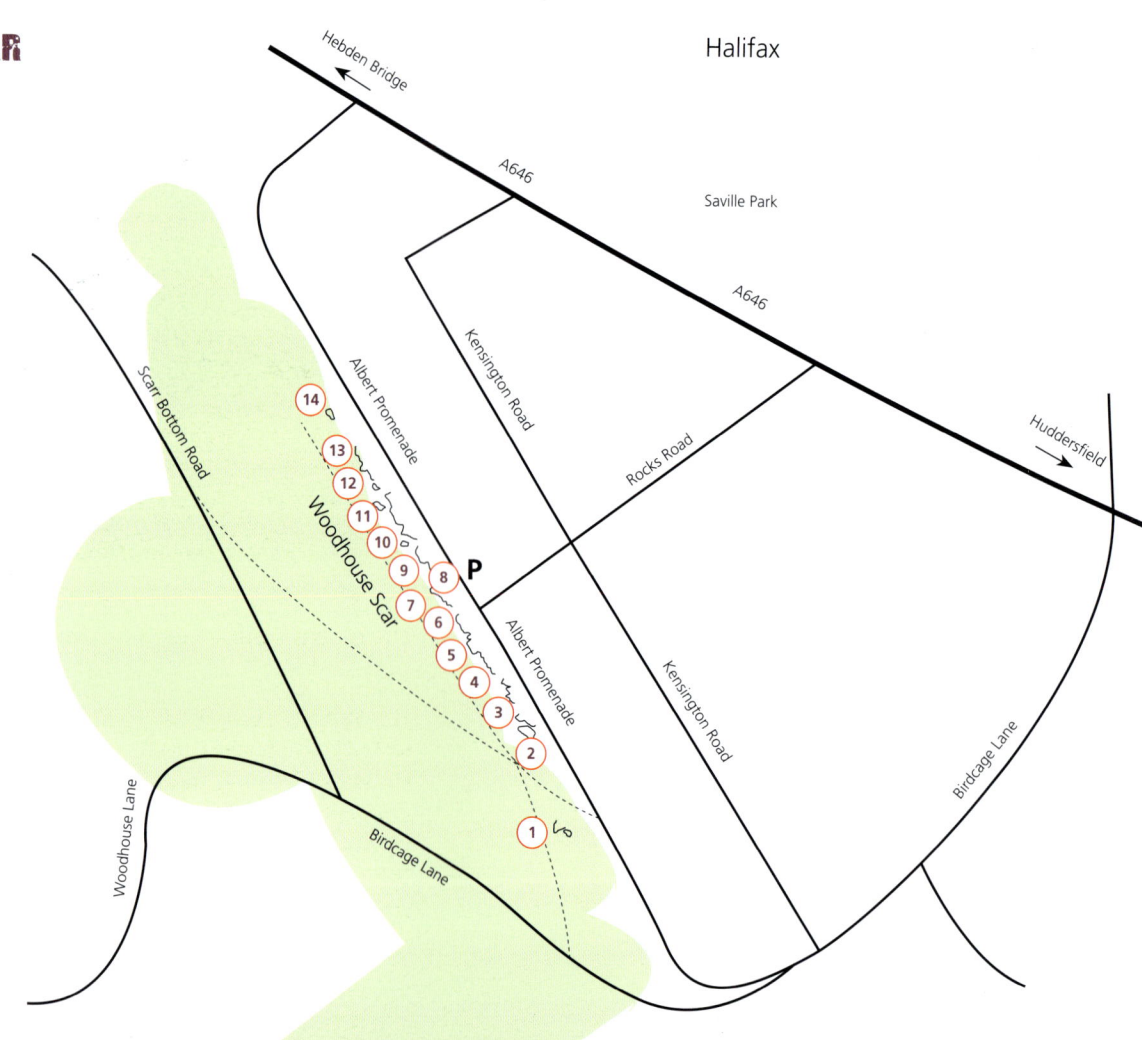

Area 1: Trackside Arete

Area 2: Trackside Boulder

1. ● (6a)
SDS. From the positive break move up left and finish up the arete.

2. ● (7a+)
SDS. From the break climb the wall above passing slopey edges. Avoid the arete.

3. ● (7a+)
L-R traverse starting on the slabby arete and finishing up problem 4.

4. ● (5+)
The wall just right of the scoop requires a dynamic approach.

1. ● (5+)
SDS. Climb the narrow nose.

2. ● (6a)
SDS. Start in the back of the roof and climb out using the corner/crack. Finish up the arete. Pulling over the roof rightwards and finishing up the centre of the wall is the same grade.

3. ● (5)
The undercut slab left of the arete.

4. ● (5+)
The right-hand arete of the slab.

5. ● (5)
SDS. Gain the block and climb the left arete of the wall.

6. ● (4)
The easy angled rampline trending leftwards.

WOOLHOUSE SCAR

293

Area 2: Trackside Boulder

1. ● (6b+)
   Technical L-R mid-height traverse. Finish up problem 5.

2. ● (4+)
   The blunt nose trending rightwards at the top.

3. ● (6a)
   The vague arete climbed on the right-hand side.

4. ● (4+)
   The thin wall just right of the vague arete.

5. ● (6a+)
   The wall passing the slot has a slopey finish.

6. ● (6a+)
   From the slot climb the wall rightwards passing a flake.

1. ● (4)
   The left side of the wall starting on the good flake.

2. ● (4+)
   The centre of the wall passing a good flake.

3. ● (6a)
   SDS. The left side of the arete. Avoid using the crack.

4. ● (4+)
   SDS. The nasty crack.

Area 3: Spire Rock

1. 🔵 (5)
Traverse L-R under the roof, swing onto the slab to finish.

2. 🟡 (6c)
The direct over the roof passing the undercut.

3. 🟡 (6c)
Traverse L-R along the lip of the roof. Finish up the arete.

1. 🟡 (6a)
The left arete to the good break. Escape.

2. 🔴 (7a+)
The wall just right of the arete passing the jagged crack. Escape at the break.

3. 🔵 (4)
The scarred wall on chipped pockets. Escape at the break.

4. 🔵 (5)
The wall left of the arete. Escape at the break.

5. 🔵 (5)
The arete avoiding the chipped edges. Escape at the break.

6. 🟡 (6a+)
The fingery wall. Avoid the arete.

Area 4: Square Face

Clingen Face is home to a huge number of eliminates. Only the none eliminate line is described here.

1. ● (7b+) Angel Face
SDS. From the corner traverse rightwards keeping low to gain the arete. Finish up on the slab.

1. ● (4+)
SDS. The left-hand side of the arete.

2. ● (5)
SDS. The right-hand side of the arete.

3. ● (6c)
The wall avoiding the arete passing slopey edges and a pocket.

4. ● (6a)
The centre of the wall via a big reach.

5. ● (4)
The left-hand side of the short arete.

Area 5: Upper Green Wall

 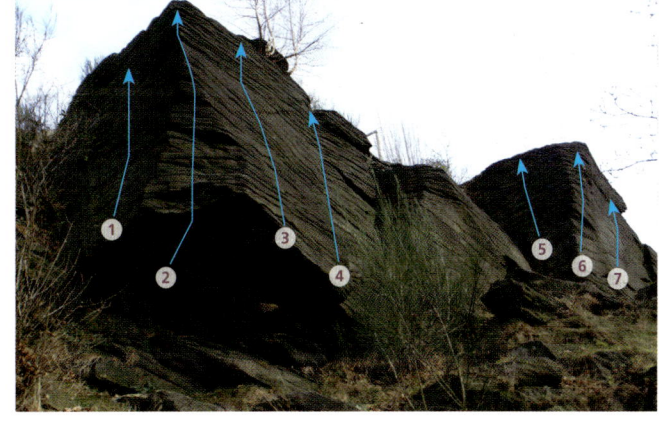

1. ● (4+)
The left-most blunt arete.

2. ● (6a+) **Radium Arete**
The undercut, green arete. SDS. Pull around the roof to join the arete for a 6c tick.

3. ● (7c) **Bear Down**
SDS. Starting just right of the arete.

4. ● (7b)
SDS. The right side of the undercut wall.

5. ● (6a)
The right edge of the wall.

6. ● (6a)
The wall passing the vertical crack.

7. ● (6a)
SDS. The blunt arete.

1. ● (4+)
The wall without the arete.

2. ● (5+)
SDS. Pull over the roof and climb the arete.

3. ● (5)
The undercut wall has a tricky start.

4. ● (5)
The right side of the wall with an awkward undercut start.

5. ● (5)
The centre of the slab.

6. ● (4)
The tiny arete just right of the wide crack/chimney.

7. ● (4)
The short wall.

8. ● (5)
The quality arete.

9. ● (5)
The wall passing good breaks.

WOOLHOUSE SCAR

297

Area 6: Poodle Wall

Area 7: Pyramid Buttress

1. ● (5)
   SDS. From the block climb the wall above.

2. ● (5+)
   Climb out from the back of the roof and finish up the arete.

3. ● (5)
   SDS. The roof crack.

4. ● (6a) **Poodle Wall**
   SDS. Climb out of the roof leftwards to the break and finish passing the pocket.

5. ● (6a+) **Poodle In Puddle**
   SDS. Climb out of the roof and finish up the arete direct.

6. ● (6b+) **Up The Poodle Without A Paddle**
   SDS. Climb out of the roof and finish up the blunt arete.

7. ● (6c) **Dog**
   SDS. Climb out of the roof and finish up the wall direct.

1. ● (4+)
   The hanging nose above the slab.

2. ● (4+)
   The right side of the nose.

3. ● (4)
   The centre of the blocky wall.

4. ● (4+)
   The steep wall left of the corner.

5. ● (6c+)
   The centre of the wall just left of an overlap.

6. ● (6c+)
   The right-hand side of the wall passing a small overlap to a positive sidepull and a stiff pull for better holds.

Area 7: Pyramid Buttress

1. ● (6a+)
   Climb the huge, undercut arete on the left-hand side.

2. ● (6a)
   The right side of the arete is marginally easier but just as terrifying.

3. ● (4+)
   The wall between the arete and the crack. Passing a pocket.

1. ● (6a)
   SDS. Climb the steep wall from low on the right.

2. ● (7a) **The Gasp**
   SDS. The undercut arete trending leftwards on juggy breaks to finish. Much easier from standing at 5.

3. ● (7a) **The Groan**
   SDS. Climb The Gasp to the break. Traverse leftwards and finish up the wall.

4. ● (5)
   The wall right of the arete.

5. ● (4)
   The big crack.

6. ● (7a) **Nobby's Piles**
   SDS. Climb the arete and pull over the roof.

Area 8: Slanting Cleft

Area 9: Piton Crack

1. ● (4+)
   The right arete of the crack.

2. ● (4+)
   The blunt arete.

3. ● (3+)
   The well-worn crack.

4. ● (5+)
   The wall avoiding the crack.

5. ● (5)
   SDS. Climb out of the small cave and finish up the wall.

1. ● (6a)
   Gain the pocket on the wall dynamically and use the arete to finish.

2. ● (7b+) **Houdini**
   SDS. From the back of the roof gain the lip and finish up the wall/arete.

3. ● (7c) **Ian's Roof** ✱
   SDS. From the back of the roof gain the lip and traverse leftwards to finish up the wall/arete.

4. ● (7b+) **Ian's Traverse**
   SDS. From the break gain the lip and traverse leftwards to finish up the wall/arete.

5. ● (7a)
   The right-hand arete climbed on the left side.

6. ● (5+)
   From the right arete traverse the wall passing pockets to finish around the arete.

Area 9: Piton Crack

1. 🔵 (4+)
   L-R traverse along the low break. Finish on the slab.

2. 🟡 (6b)
   L-R traverse of the high break. Finish up the arete.

3. 🟡 (6c) **Piton Crack** ✳
   The highball crack requires a committed approach. SDS. 6c.

4. 🟡 (6a+)
   The highball, undercut arete. Tackled on the left-hand side.

Dalvinder Sodhi warming up at Woodhouse Scar: Steve Dunning

Area 10: Overhanging Group

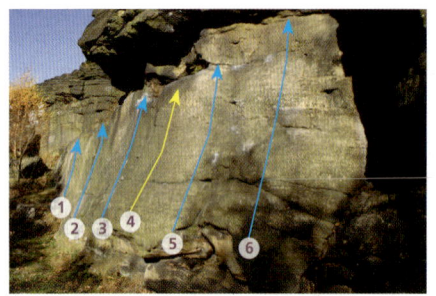  

1. ● (4+)
   The chipped slab left of the crack. Avoid the crack.

2. ● (4+)
   SDS. The crack.

3. ● (5+)
   The wall right of the crack. Escape at the roof.

4. ● (4)
   The prominent groove. Escape at the roof.

5. ● (6c+)
   Eliminate wall right of the groove. Avoiding the groove.

6. ● (5+)
   Climb the wall to the roof. Escape.

1. ● (4)
   The corner crack. Escape at the roof rightwards.

2. ● (6b+)
   The small arete is superb.

3. ● (5+)
   The undercut arete.

1. ● (5+)
   The undercut rib.

2. ● (6a)
   SDS. The blunt rib.

3. ● (5)
   The steep wall just right of the corner.

Area 11: Pebble Buttress

Area 12: Cave Buttress

1. ● (5)
The hanging arete. A bit close to the gully.

2. ● (6a+)
The centre of the wall.

3. ● (4+)
The arete of the detached block.

4. ● (3+)
The easy face on the detached block.

5. ● (7a+)
The thin wall just right of the block.

6. ● (6b)
SDS. Starting on the right climb the wall passing a slot. Climb leftwards and finish through the roof above 'Chris' graffiti.

7. ● (6a) **Cave Crack Direct**
The short crack.

1. ● (6a)
The wall between the groove and the blunt arete. SDS. Starting on a flake under the roof is worth 6a+.

2. ● (6b+)
SDS. Pull over the roof. Finish up the rib.

3. ● (6a) **Johnny One Time**
The wall just right of the blunt rib. SDS. 6b+.

4. ● (4)
The easy angled wall right of the blunt rib passing a big pocket/slot.

5. ● (6b+)
SDS. Pull around the lip and climb the wall just left of the arete.

WOOLHOUSE SCAR

303

Area 12: Cave Buttress

Area 13: Slab Buttress

1. 🔵 (4)
   The left arete of the scooped slab.

2. 🟡 (6c+) **Done Years Ago**
   The left side of the scooped wall.

3. 🟡 (6a) **Metal Mickey**
   The wall just left of the corner. Avoid the right wall.

4. 🟡 (6b+)
   SDS. From the base of the crack crank up rightwards to the top break. Traverse the break to the right arete.

5. 🟡 (6c)
   Start as for problem 4. From the mid-height break traverse rightwards to finish around the arete.

6. 🔵 (5+)
   The left side of the wall passing the groove.

1. 🔵 (5+)
   SDS. The blunt arete/nose.

2. 🔵 (4)
   The wall just right of the left arete/nose.

3. 🟡 (6c)
   SDS. Eliminate. Just use the seam.

4. 🔵 (5)
   The crack.

Area 14: The Sheriff

1. ● (3+)
   The left side of the easy angled slab.
2. ● (4)
   The slab to the right avoiding the good holds.
3. ● (3+)
   The slab passing good pockets.

1. ● (6c)
   The centre of the wall passing the slopers to a tricky mantle.

The block to the right offers a thuggy mantle problem at around 5. The slab right again has a number of possibilities all of which are easy.

1. ● (6c)
   SDS. The finger crack is climbed from the back of the roof. Get crawling.
2. ● (7b+) **Mango**
   SDS. From the back of the roof climb out to the diagonal crack aqnd finish leftwards. Hard for the grade.
3. ● (7b/+) **The Sheriff**
   SDS. Climb out from the back of the roof. Finish via the diagonal crack. With or without the arete the grade is the same.

- Bolt-on holds
- Training boards
- Bouldering Walls
- Leading Walls
- Mobile Towers
- Ice Walls
- Artificial caves

Entre-Prises (UK) Ltd
T: 01282 444800   F: 01282 444801
info@ep-uk.com   www.entre-prises.com

Partner to the British Mountaineering Council & International Federation of Sport Climbing

Photo: Craggy Island

TOTAL-CLIMBING

YORKSHIRE GRITSTONE BOULDERING
Volume 2, February 2008

Photo: Alex Messenger

Notes: